C000142265

The Garden Maker's
Book of Wonder

The GARDEN MAKER'S
Book of Wonder

ALLISON VALLIN KOSTOVICK
CREATOR OF Finch + Folly

Storey Publishing

The mission of Storey Publishing is to serve our customers by
publishing practical information that encourages
personal independence in harmony with the environment.

Edited by Carleen Madigan
Art direction and book design by Erin Dawson
Text production by Liseann Karandisecky

Cover photography by © Stacey Cramp, front, back
(t. & 2nd f.t.); © Allison Vallin Kostovick,
back (b. & 2nd f.b.)

Interior photography by © Allison Vallin Kostovick,
except for © Stacey Cramp, i–iii, vi, viii, 6, 8 t., 9,
20 b.l., 26, 28 t., 30, 33 t., 42 t.r., 45 l., 46, 50, 58, 59,
61 b., 65 b.r., 66, 70–72, 73 m.r., 75, 83, 84, 93 t.l., 94,
96, 98, 99, 102, 111 b., 112 t., 116 b., 118, 121 b., 126 t.l. &
b.r., 131 t., 133 r., 135, 137 t.l., 140, 146, 148, 153 b., 161,
162, 164, 167 b., 168, 171 b., 172, 173 t., 178, 179, 184, 188,
190 b.c., 193 t., 198, 199, 206, 209 t.r., 210, 218, 221 t.,
222, 223, 228, 229, 231, 233–236, 244–246

Additional photography by © INTREEGUE
Photography/Shutterstock, 77 b.c.; © Malivan_Iuliia/
Shutterstock, 77 t. 2nd from l.; Mars Vilaubi © Storey
Publishing, LLC, 33 b., 90, 109 t.

Illustrations by © Enya Todd, except for © Allison
Vallin Kostovick, 9, 12, 18, 37, 45, 49 (l.), 57, 74, 87,
96, 138, 142, 148, 159, 163, 192, 200, 210, 231

Icons by © Allison Vallin Kostovick, 43 and throughout, 65 and throughout; Erin Dawson © Storey
Publishing, LLC, 9 and throughout, 15 and throughout, 17 and throughout

Text © 2023 by Allison Vallin Kostovick

All rights reserved. No part of this book may be reproduced without written permission from the publisher,
except by a reviewer who may quote brief passages or
reproduce illustrations in a review with appropriate
credits; nor may any part of this book be reproduced,
stored in a retrieval system, or transmitted in any form
or by any means—electronic, mechanical, photocopy-
ing, recording, or other—without written permission
from the publisher.

The information in this book is true and complete
to the best of our knowledge. All recommendations
are made without guarantee on the part of the author
or Storey Publishing. The author and publisher dis-
claim any liability in connection with the use of this
information.

The publisher is not responsible for websites (or
their content) that are not owned by the publisher.

Storey books are available at special discounts
when purchased in bulk for premiums and sales
promotions as well as for fund-raising or educa-
tional use. Special editions or book excerpts can
also be created to specification. For details, please
send an email to special.markets@hbgusa.com.

Storey Publishing
210 MASS MoCA Way
North Adams, MA 01247
storey.com

Storey Publishing, LLC is an imprint of Workman
Publishing Co., Inc., a subsidiary of Hachette Book
Group, Inc., 1290 Avenue of the Americas, New York,
NY 10104

ISBNs: 978-1-63586-531-8 (hardcover);
978-1-63586-532-5 (ebook)

Printed in China by R. R. Donnelley
10 9 8 7 6 5 4 3 2 1

Library of Congress Cataloging-in-Publication
Data on file

For my Tom

Together we sowed the first seeds of this beautiful life together, and how wonderfully it has bloomed. Thank you for being you and for your endless love and support. You are my heart.

For my sons, Jackson and Boyd

All my love always and forever.

For my Cobbs

My constant companion in and out of the garden. You truly have been a dream come true.

CONTENTS

Summer A Time to Do 67

Autumn   A Time to Reflect   125

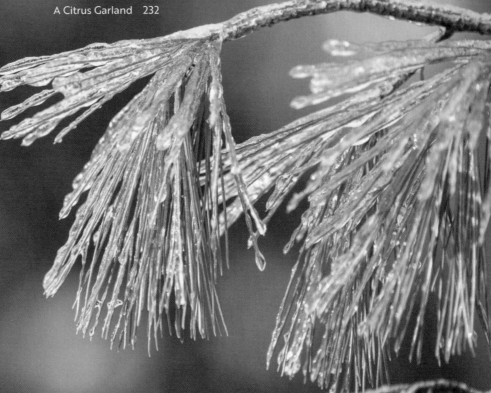

Winter   A Time to Rest 177

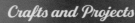

Growing Everyday Magic

YOU MAY HAVE HEARD THE TERM "EVERYDAY MAGIC," but how often do you truly see it? I have to say, I see it every day, throughout the day, and that has made all the difference in how I live, and, frankly, in the quality of my life.

I'll always remember the day my perspective changed. I was having a horrible day—just a completely frustrating, aggravating, all the "-atings" kind of day. And I just needed to get out of the house. So I grabbed my camera and started to walk up the road. This only depressed me more, for it was late November and everything was either dead or some shade of brown. As I walked, I laughed at myself for even bringing my camera . . . there was nothing worth capturing. So my bad attitude and I turned around, crossed the street, and headed home.

That's when I stumbled upon a kind of pinecone I hadn't seen before. When I bent down to pick it up, I noticed in the near distance a patch of winterberry growing by a swampy area behind the crumbling stone wall. I then spied the coolest crystal formation in the frozen patch of a puddle. Framed well with my camera lens, it would make for a magical capture, so I started snapping away. Almost in an instant, my perspective changed. Those dull brown leaves were surprisingly full of intricate veining when I gave them a closer look. All the things I had disregarded as dead really weren't. On closer inspection, each object was brimming with different kinds of beauty—subtle ones, the type you would never notice unless you slowed down and made a point to look. I returned from my walk invigorated, frustration-free, and so very grateful to nature for guiding me to see beyond my short-view vision of the world.

It's easy to find beauty and inspiration when they are obvious, but to allow yourself to slow down and observe your surroundings—to simply be present—is truly everything. It sounds so darn simple to do! And in theory it is. But the magic lies in putting it into practice. Welcoming a bit of "everyday magic" into your day will help you relish your garden and surroundings, but it will also be a panacea of sorts for all that may ail you in life. Forging a deeper connection with nature will affect your approach to gardening and your perspective on life. The result will be harvests not only for the belly but for the soul and mind as well. Allow yourself to enjoy your garden journey, and sow the seeds to growing your own everyday magic.

I hope this book can serve as an introduction to simple ways you can celebrate garden life and nature all year long. Inside you'll find growing tips, projects, and recipes that have lifted up my garden heart the most over these past 25 years of growing. A beautiful, exciting journey lies ahead. May you embark with enthusiasm and kindness and let nature nourish your soul.

Allison Vallin Kostovick

Spring

A Time to Sow

For folks in northern climates, the buildup to spring is a slow beat of excitement that steadily grows louder over the advancing weeks, until one day we glance out the window and are greeted by sights we had only dreamed about for the past few months. As the last patch of snow melts, the woods, its inhabitants, the garden, and I shed our heavy hibernation sweaters and celebrate the arrival of a new season.

When you live in a colder climate, spring really is something to rejoice in—you simply can't help but celebrate. It awakens your senses from their winter slumber, sending them into overload. The landscape ebbs from a snowy white and flows into a patchwork of vivid greens. Winter's still quiet is banished as a chorus of peepers and robins fills the air. With every step, bright, inviting scents and textures beckon to be sniffed and touched. Everything is brand new again. And anything is possible.

Spring Thoughts for a
New Growing Season

Once upon a time in my garden journey, my springs were a combination of complete and utter excitement balanced with all-out fretting. I used to think that the starting dates on seed packets were fairly loose recommendations (they're not) and that I knew better (I didn't). I was convinced that bigger seedlings were better seedlings—so I started my tomatoes in February, not late March as advised for my region, and ended up with 4-foot-tall tomato trees . . . I mean *seedlings*. I also sowed my flower seeds a good 3 to 4 weeks earlier than I should have, only to watch them sadly attempt to bloom under the grow lights in my living room.

It took a combination of learning the hard way and putting hours and hours of research into practice to learn that I really needed to relax and slow down. These days, I start my seeds at a more sensible time. Not only has that helped my seedlings, it's helped my sanity, as I've freed up for myself the time and energy it took to care for all those plants indoors for that long.

Have Patience

The very first seed I ever sowed broke my gardening heart—then turned around and saved it.

It was the first summer my husband and I spent in the first home we had ever rented. Knowing nothing about gardening but overflowing with enthusiasm, I bought a packet of forget-me-not seeds and tenderly sowed my very first seeds in a pot on the stairs of our back deck. Throughout the summer, with lots of love and care, that pot flourished, producing a grand flush of leaves. I couldn't wait to see it in bloom! But waiting is what I did that entire summer. I continued to care for that big pot of leaves, in optimistic hope that a peep of blue would emerge. But as frost was about to nip and there was still no sign of a flower, I was heartbroken—and frankly a bit miffed at this whole gardening thing.

Knowing that the growing season was now over and nothing would come of that well-tended plant, I grabbed the big pot of leaves and hurled it with all my might into the woods behind our house. In that moment, I literally wiped my hands of gardening. I was done. All that care and love and hope. For what? A pot of leaves?

The following spring, as I stood out on our back deck, a twinkle of the brightest sparkling blue caught my eye. I ran into the woods to see what it was and was greeted by a patch of the most enchanting tiny blue flowers I had ever seen. It took me a few minutes to piece together that those blue beauties were none other than that pot of forget-me-nots I had hurled into the woods. Talk about a humbling moment! I had forgotten them, but they hadn't forgotten me.

That was my great "a-ha" moment. It was my first lesson in gardening, but it was also the first of many life lessons that gardening has taught me: not only to never give up, but also to educate myself (and that nature is a magical teacher!). That forget-me-not failing to bloom the first year caused me to embark on a whole new quest for knowledge that unlocked one door after the next. I learned that this charming flower wasn't supposed to bloom its first year—that it's a perennial. Then I learned what a perennial was. And only then did I learn that my first seed-sowing experience was a success after all.

I am forever grateful for that forget-me-not. I'm thankful every day for the lesson in patience and optimism it taught me; that's been the secret to why I'm still gardening all these years later.

Work with Nature

The day I fully embraced practicing permaculture was the day I learned to grow with the flow, which has brought a level of peace and calm to gardening that I didn't even know I needed until I had it.

Permaculture is a way of working with the nature around you, rather than against it. It's a sustainable, mutually beneficial approach that takes into consideration not only the needs of the gardener but of the garden itself, as well as all the creatures around it. This creates harmony in the garden, providing a natural balance that frees you up for more frolicking and less working.

The growing advice you'll read throughout this book follows the practices of permaculture: techniques like crop rotation, companion planting, using native plants, planting in hügelkultur mounds, no-till cultivation, and composting.

The Key to Organic Success Is in the Soil

Much of the key to garden success lies in the health of the soil. Healthy garden soil is nutrient and mineral rich and retains its water content well. A good indicator of happy soil is earthworms. These wriggling friends are a sign that you have loose, fertile soil, and the worms in turn contribute to the upkeep of the soil's health with their castings—a gift of compost gold. If you're not seeing a lot of worms, add a 6- to 10-inch layer of compost or organic mulch on top of your garden soil.

Diversity Is a Cornerstone in a Balanced Garden

You can have the best gardening practices in the world, but at the end of the day, you're at the mercy of Mother Nature and her weather wand. Often the key to garden success is to grow a wide variety of crops, knowing that

some will do well over the course of a season while others will do okay at best. Those wet summers, which spread fungal diseases to tomatoes and peppers, are the very same summers your root veggies grow their very best. During drought years, our onion and carrot harvests were dismal, but we had our best cabbage, lavender, and beans ever.

Planting a diverse array of crops also mitigates the ability of one pest or disease to do widespread damage. Diversity extends beyond vegetables. By incorporating flowers and herbs into your garden, you'll attract a wider range of beneficial insects, which in turn help with pest control and increase the pollination rate of your vegetables.

Native Plants for Less Work

Enjoy your garden more and toil less by incorporating more native plants into the mix. These low-maintenance plants are adapted to thrive in your environment while providing an important food and shelter source for native pollinators and wildlife. Come spring, look around your community for native plant sales. Organizations like the National Audubon Society and your local university Cooperative Extension Service often host these events. They're great places to pick up some of these valuable garden partners.

LADY FERN

TALL WHITE ASTER

GOLDENROD

Bees forage for pollen on the flowers of borage (shown here) and mallow (below).

Be a Pollinator's Pal

At first, the thought of sharing valuable growing space with a crop that isn't edible didn't seem to make much sense to me.

But incorporating flowers into my vegetable garden caused a magical transformation. Not only did the landscape dance with hues I'd never seen in my garden, but the garden itself literally came alive. With the flowers came an army of pollinators and beneficial insects zipping, flying, buzzing, and flitting across every inch of the garden. Today, my garden is so alive with insects, birds, and wildlife that I realize it isn't my garden at all anymore . . . it's theirs. And that's truly transformational for all.

A Pollinator Playground

Create your own pollinator playground, rich with beneficial insects and critters of all sorts, and make your garden the place to BEE with these ways to beckon pollinators.

◆ **You've got to be single to mingle.** Pollinators prefer single blossoms, which offer more nectar and easier access to pollen than double blooms do.

◆ **There's gold in the old.** Choose native and heirloom plants, as these varieties produce the most pollen.

◆ **Think seasonally.** Try to arrange your garden plantings so that you can offer your pollinator pals nonstop flowers from spring to fall.

◆ **Let nature take the wheel.** Let plant volunteers grow with abandon, and leave some logs and fresh water in a wild patch somewhere nearby for pollinator nesting and napping.

ALLIUM

BEE BALM

GLOBE GILIA

SALVIA

SUNFLOWER

OREGANO

A Few Favorite
BEE-FRIENDLY BLOOMS

Allium

Anise hyssop

Aster

Bee balm

Butterfly bush

Echinacea

Globe gilia

Goldenrod

Phlox

Pincushion flower

Rudbeckia

Runner beans

Salvia

Sunflower

Sweet alyssum

Yarrow

Zinnia

Flowering herbs like oregano,
thyme, and sage

Garden Volunteers

I could wax poetic about the merits of plants that self-sow, but for now here are three favorite traits.

☀ **Instant whimsy.** If you want that wild garden look, full of beckoning blooms in every nook and cranny, then let some of your favorite flowers go to seed at the end of the season. Come next spring, nature will step in and take it from there.

☀ **Instant bounty of vibrant, healthy plants guaranteed to thrive in your garden.** When I grow larkspur myself, the plants are okay at best, with only one or two branches of flowers. It wasn't until larkspur volunteers started sprouting up that I learned how incredibly gorgeous, strong, and vibrant these flowers could be: tall, strapping plants, bearing many branches of beautiful flowers in shades of purple, pink, and white.

☀ **An effortless way to grow edible flowers.** A plethora of violas, nasturtiums, and chive blossoms sprinkled across a big bowl of garden-fresh greens transforms the dish from a simple salad to a showstopping feast for the eyes and belly in seconds.

A few of my favorite volunteers include anise hyssop, baby's breath, borage, calendula, catnip, chamomile, chives, coriander, cornflowers, dill, echinacea, feverfew, foxglove, globe gilia, larkspur, lemon balm, linaria, love-in-a-mist, nasturtiums, nicotiana, pansies, catchfly, rose campion, sunflowers, and violas.

DILL

VIOLAS

CHIVE BLOSSOMS

LARKSPUR

13

YOUNG LILAC LEAVES

MAPLE LEAVES

LILAC FLOWERS

FORSYTHIA

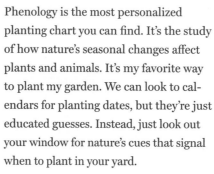

Planting to Phenology

Phenology is the most personalized planting chart you can find. It's the study of how nature's seasonal changes affect plants and animals. It's my favorite way to plant my garden. We can look to calendars for planting dates, but they're just educated guesses. Instead, just look out your window for nature's cues that signal when to plant in your yard.

When lilac bushes leaf out, sow lettuce. Once they're in bloom, sow annual flowers, beans, and squash. When flowers fade, sow cucumbers.

CROCUS

Favorite Seasonal Cues

* When forsythia blooms, plant peas and onions, and prune roses.

* Plant perennials when maple trees begin to leaf out. When maple leaves unfurl, sow morning glories.

* Are dandelions and crocuses blooming? Start sowing carrots, lettuce, beets, and spinach.

* When daylilies and lily of the valley start blooming and apple blossoms begin to drift to the ground, it's time to plant tomatoes, pole beans, corn, and peppers.

* Peonies blossoming? That's a green light to get melons in the ground.

* Plant corn when oak leaves are as big as a squirrel's ears.

Protecting Your Chickens from Predators

With the arrival of spring comes the need to keep a watchful eye on hens. Spring tends to be peak predator time. Some, like hawks, are looking for food. Others, like raccoons, are teaching their babes how to hunt. My being diligent about springing into action at each chicken shriek has thankfully prevented any losses in more than a dozen years of raising chickens. Decking out the coop and run with some of the following items has also helped keep them safe.

◆ Use a tall fence and trench it a foot into the ground. This prevents predators from digging under or climbing over into the coop.

◆ String reflective tape across the top of the run. This prevents hawks from flying into the coop. Hanging old CDs or DVDs has a similar effect.

◆ Keep a radio playing somewhere by the coop to ward off pests.

◆ When in doubt, a wok and a rock do the job. In other words, have something loud nearby to clang to scare off intruders.

Tips for Germinating Seeds

Some seeds need help in waking from dormancy in order to germinate. Many tiny seeds crave light, so it's best not to cover them when sowing. Other seeds with tough outer coatings, like beans, are helped by a 12-hour soak to soften that shell and make it easier for germination to occur. Know before you sow and increase your germination rates.

Seeds that need light to germinate: Alyssum, bee balm, begonia, coleus, columbine, dill, geranium, impatiens, lettuce, nicotiana, petunia, poppy, snapdragon, and violas (among others!). Sow on top of and gently press into the soil, but don't cover.

Seeds that need darkness to germinate: Calendula, cornflowers, and delphinium.

Seeds that need a nick before sowing: Hibiscus, marshmallow, passionflower, pumpkins, and squash. Like peas and beans, these have a tough outer seed coat. You can soak the seeds to soften them. Alternatively, use sandpaper or a knife to gently scratch the seed coat, which creates an opening for the seedling to emerge through (this is called scarification).

Seeds that need a soak: Beans, beets, peas, and sweet peas. Their hard outer coating can make it difficult for the seedling to break through. Soak for 12 to 24 hours prior to sowing to soften the seed shell and improve germination.

Seeds that need cold: Anise hyssop, arugula, brassica family, carrots, catmint, coneflower, larkspur, lavender, leeks, lettuce, lupine, milkweed, onion, peas, rudbeckia, scabiosa, and spinach. These seeds need to be exposed to a period of cold before they can germinate (this is called cold stratification). How cold and for how long depends on the plant. Most just need to be put in the refrigerator for a few weeks prior to sowing.

 GROW

Let the Seed Color Guide You

When direct sowing in spring, seed color can give you a hint as to when to plant. Some varieties of lettuce and beans have dark seeds, while the seeds of other varieties are very light. Those lighter-colored seeds crave warmer soil temperature than their darker counterparts do. If the temperature is too cool, this could crack their coating, which reduces the germination rate. For best results, wait until the soil warms to 70°F/21°C before you sow light seeds.

Thinning Seedlings,
Even If You Don't Want To

Is there any more painful job in gardening than thinning seedlings? Picture trays of fat, happy seedlings that all germinated with much better success than you expected. Picture that plug of zinnias bursting with three plants, when you know a plug should contain only one. Trimming extra seedlings is gut-wrenching. Yet it absolutely must be done for the best chance at seedling success. Otherwise you run the risk of spindly, weak plants that may not handle transplanting well. And don't try to be like me in my early days, when I'd gently tease out the superfluous seedling (roots and all) and try to transplant it into its own container. Sure, I had good intentions, but in reality, I was disturbing their delicate root system, shocking the seedlings. It's best if you just use clean scissors (emphasis on *clean*; you can easily spread disease otherwise) to snip off the extra seedlings.

 EAT

To ease the pain of thinning, feast on a celebratory first harvest of the season made from all the little lopped-off seedlings. It'll be the perfect appetizer to kick off your springtime feast.

17

Pointers for Potting Up

Once your seeds have germinated and the seedlings have developed two or three sets of leaves, it's time to pot them up. You can pretty much grow plants in anything as long as it's clean. Your choices can be as budget friendly as repurposing yogurt containers and milk jugs, making your own soil blocks, or folding pots out of newspaper. Make sure to poke some drainage holes into any container with a solid bottom.

Some plants are picky about their containers. Squash, pumpkins, cucumbers, peas, and beans do not like having their roots disturbed. It's best to sow those in biodegradable containers that can be planted directly in the ground. Other plants, like corn and sweet peas, prefer narrow, deep pots that support their roots.

When selecting the pot, avoid the temptation to put a small seedling in a big pot. Rather, you want to start small, usually potting up a germinated seedling into a 3-inch container. As the plant grows, you may need to pot up once again to allow the root system to continue to grow healthily and prevent it from becoming rootbound. When potting up again, select the next pot size up from the one you're currently using.

Soil choice is very important at this stage. Seed-starting soil is great for germinating your seeds, but when it's time to pot up seedlings, you'll want to use a good-quality potting mix rich in soil, compost, coir, and sand or perlite. This combination not only offers needed nutrients but allows for good water retention and airflow. A quality potting mix provides seedlings with the nutrients they need at this stage to grow strong. Once in their new containers, you can give seedlings a drink of diluted organic plant food.

Easing Seedlings into the Garden

A few weeks before transplanting into the garden, the great seedling migration begins. Your seedlings are going to need a slow transition from the comforts of your home into the "real world" of the garden. Find a sheltered spot out of strong winds and sun, and bring your seedlings outside, starting with just a few hours outdoors each day and gradually building up their exposure time over the course of a week or two. This hardens off your seedlings, reducing the risk of transplant shock and easing their transition to the outside world.

Pinch Me!

Some plants benefit greatly from a good haircut or pinching back at seedling stage.

Give **onions** a well-deserved haircut when they reach 6 inches tall so they develop bigger, thicker, stronger necks. Using clean, sharp shears, cut the seedlings back to 3 inches in height. Depending how long until transplanting time, you may need to give them another trim somewhere down the line.

When **cosmos** and **zinnia** seedlings are 8 to 10 inches tall, pinch back the top 3 inches of the plant. This creates a bushier, more prolific plant.

Herbs like **basil, oregano, thyme,** and **mint** morph into a large mass of delicious leaves when kept pinched back.

When **dahlias** have their first few sets of leaves, pinch them back. This will create a well-branched plant, which means lots more captivating blooms. If your pinched-off stems are solid (they become hollow as they grow bigger), dip them in rooting hormone and pot up. A month down the road, each pinched-off top should have a strong, vibrant root system ready for transplanting.

Did you know that most growth hormones in **hot pepper** plants live in the tip-top portion of the plant? By pinching off the top, you signal to the plant to focus its energy on branching out rather than growing taller. This leads to a more productive, sturdier plant chock-full of peppers. Top when the plant has had a chance to develop a few sets of leaves and a good root system. Since topping off does shock the system a bit initially, the plant will need a few days to a week to rebound. After that, you'll start to see leaves sprouting from the side nodes of the stem.

Garden Architecture

Vertical gardening—growing up trellises, poles, or archways—adds so much more to your garden than just valuable growing space. Incorporating this kind of garden architecture adds instant whimsy and personality to your layout, especially in spring when the garden looks a bit naked and flat.

The material you choose for trellises really sets the mood for your garden. I love to use branches, not only because I live in the woods and they're plentiful, but also because they bring a storybook quality to my garden that I relish. But you can achieve the same effect with bamboo poles, shepherd hooks, or pretty much anything around your home that can be repurposed—like that old ladder no one uses anymore. How pretty would that be standing proudly in the garden, each rung brimming over with morning glories and cucumbers?

GROW

Going Vertical

Here are things to keep in mind when considering a vertical setup.

◆ Select materials that can support the weight of the crop that will be trellised. For example, hefty tomato plants require a lot more support than flowering vines or beans.

◆ Short on garden space? Try adding a trellis to a barrel planter, a 15-gallon fabric grow bag, or a large pot.

◆ When planning where to place your vertical elements, be mindful of not blocking the sun for neighboring plants. It's best to install architectural pieces on the north end of your garden so they don't block any of those gorgeous rays.

◆ Some materials last longer than others. After 2 years in the garden, most of my branched trellises have become too brittle to properly support plants, so those get replaced often. But the cattle fencing used for my archways is going strong 5 years in and looks to have many more years of service.

◆ When tying plants to your verticals, use jute twine whenever possible, leaving a few inches of string hanging after the knot. Birds love perching high on trellises and will actively visit to nip strands of jute for building their nests.

Varieties Matter

It took me many, many years of growing failures before I realized that when it comes to selecting varieties to grow, I need to read beyond the dreamy seed catalog descriptions. Not all varieties grow well in all hardiness zones.

These plants are ones I used to struggle with. After discovering the best variety for my zone, though, they're now some of the most vigorous plants I grow.

Sage

Common sage has been one of my most prolific perennial herbs, taking our Maine winters in stride. Other varieties, like pineapple sage and variegated sage, are much more tender; in colder areas, grow these as annuals.

Thyme

We gardeners often think of thyme as a perennial, then fret we did something wrong when the plant fails to return the following spring. Turns out, different varieties are hardy to certain zones. German/winter thyme is a great perennial for Zones 5 to 9, but French and lemon thymes aren't as hardy and are best grown as annuals in colder climates.

Lavender

While the woods of Maine may not offer the ideal conditions for these Mediterranean beauties, growing lavender here is feasible. Sticking with English lavender, as opposed to French and Spanish varieties, is key. I've found my best success with 'Hidcote' and 'Munstead' varieties. They successfully handle our Zone 5b cold and don't mind overwintering under lots of snow.

Rosemary

Much like its Mediterranean cousin lavender, rosemary doesn't exactly beg to be grown in my woodland setting, and although it can be grown only as an annual in Maine, it's too fabulous an herb to be without. Varieties like 'Arp', 'Madeline Hill', and 'Salem' fare better in colder climates.

Onions

When it comes to selecting onions, geography matters. Onion bulbing is dependent on day length. Growers in lower latitudes should look for short-day varieties, while northern growers should stick with long-day or intermediate-day onions.

Sweet Peas

Like onions, sweet peas require a certain day length to achieve growing success. There are short- and long-day varieties, as well as neutral options. 'Spencer Mix' varieties need 12 hours of sun each day to bloom, whereas 'Early Multiflora' varieties require only 10 hours of daylight.

Asparagus

Asparagus plants are dioecious, which means they produce both male and female plants. I learned the hard way that there's a big difference between female and male asparagus when I grew the heirloom variety 'Mary Washington'. That variety consistently produces 80 percent female plants, which are so busy making seeds that their stalks are much smaller than the males'. The males also produce three times more stalks! So, for best results, grow male-only hybrids.

PEAS

Be warned, these tasty little orbs of happiness can lead to acts of greediness and hoarding if there aren't plenty around to share, so please try to grow as many as possible.

WHEN TO SOW
Direct seed as early as the soil can be worked.

SOIL
Compost-rich, with good drainage

PREFERRED LIGHT
Part shade

Tips + Tricks

GROWING

◆ Companion plant with beans and corn. Foes are onions and garlic.

◆ Sow varieties with smooth pea seeds in early spring, as they're more cold tolerant than wrinkled ones. Save the wrinkled seeds to sow later in the season. (Wrinkled seeds also indicate sweeter-tasting varieties.)

◆ Let pea roots feed the soil. Once your harvest is done, don't uproot the plants; instead, cut off each vine at its base, leaving the roots in the ground to return nitrogen to the soil.

◆ Succession plant with cucumbers. They thrive off the nitrogen peas leave behind.

◆ Sow in autumn as well as in spring. Sow 8 weeks before your first frost date (this may work best for folks in cooler climates). Keep the seeds well watered for good germination. You won't get the same abundance as in spring sowings, but the cooler days help peas retain their bright and fresh sweetness.

HARVESTING

◆ Harvest snow peas while the pods are immature and flat.

◆ Take the garden heat out of your peas and retain their sweet happiness by dunking them in cold water immediately after harvest. Dry them well and refrigerate in plastic bags.

EATING

◆ Eat peas soon after harvesting. Shortly after peas are picked, the sugars that make them so yummy quickly turn into starch. If you can't nosh on them right on the spot, store them in a plastic bag in the refrigerator for up to 3 days.

Favorite Varieties

Sow early, mid-season, and late varieties for a full season of sweetness.

SHELL: 'Iona Petit Pois', 'Lincoln', 'Green Arrow', 'Wando'

SNOW: 'Carouby de Maussane', 'Green Beauty', 'Oregon Sugar', 'Golden Sweet'

SNAP: 'Sugar Ann', 'Opal Creek'

Pea tendrils and leaves are edible as well.

'CAROUBY DE MAUSSANE' SNOW PEA BLOSSOM

'BLAUWSCHOKKER'

Sugar snap peas are at their tastiest when harvested about a week after flowering.

✕ EAT

CRISPY MINT & PEAS

Fried, crispy mint leaves tossed with sautéed peas is a whole lot of happy for your taste buds. Heat a small amount of vegetable oil to 325°F/170°C. Drop in the leaves, just a few at a time. Cook for 30 seconds, then flip them over and cook for an additional 30 seconds. Remove and place on a paper towel. The mint leaves will dry to a crisp finish, keeping their bright green color. If they brown, it's a sign the oil may be too hot. Toss with lightly steamed or sautéed peas and finish with a sprinkling of salt.

FAVAS

Beautiful broad beans are a treat for you and your soil. Favas are so good for building healthy soil that they are sometimes known more as a cover crop than as a beloved garden veggie. But you're missing out if you don't take full advantage of this gorgeous and delicious bean.

WHEN TO SOW
Direct sow as early as the soil can be worked; favas prefer cool weather.

SOIL
Compost-rich, with good drainage

PREFERRED LIGHT
Full sun

Tips + Tricks

GROWING

- Companion plant with carrots, lettuce, peas, cabbage, and potatoes.

- Pinch off the tip of the plant as soon as you spy beans developing at the base. This concentrates the plant's energy on developing large pods. Make sure to eat those pinched-off tops—they're delicious steamed or sautéed.

- Help prevent damage from blackflies by removing the tip of the plant as soon as young pods begin to appear. Blackflies' favorite treats are the young, tender leaves that form at the tip of fava beans.

- Keep the plants well watered during dry spells. The plants crave moist, but not wet, soil, especially during flowering and pod development. If too dry, both blossoms and pods will drop.

HARVESTING

- Harvest from the base up. If you pick favas young, you can eat the whole pod. Or wait until the pods thicken up, fat with bulging beans, then pop the beans out of the shell, in the same manner you would with edamame, for noshing.

- After harvesting the pods, cut back the plant to just above a leaf node so that only a 5- to 6-inch stalk remains. Depending on your growing zone, this cutting back may spur a second flush of beans.

- Leave the stalk. Even if you don't get a second flush of beans, you'll want the stalk to stay in the soil. Favas add more nitrogen to the soil than they use (which, incidentally, makes them a wonderful crop to sow after heavy feeders like tomatoes). As the stalk slowly decomposes, it releases all that valuable nitrogen into your garden bed.

Favorite Varieties

'Windsor', 'Extra Precoce a Grano Violetto', 'Vroma', 'Robin Hood'

These stalks of white blossoms kissed with black blotches are striking when used in borders or mixed with herbs and flowers.

EAT

GRILLED BROAD BEANS

I admit to growing favas simply to eat them grilled. I became obsessed with grilling the pods whole after being surprised by how a bean that comes in this huge pod and large shell reveals itself to be pretty tiny once its casings are removed. Rather than go through the cumbersome shelling process, I simply take the whole pods, give them a quick drizzle of olive oil, season with salt and pepper, and toss them onto the grill. Once the pods are charred, they're done. Nosh on them like edamame, popping the beans straight into your mouth. Pure heaven!

SPRING

27

Snip off the greens right above the root immediately after harvesting. This helps keep the radishes crisp by allowing them to retain their water content.

'CHERRY BELLE' (LEFT), 'FRENCH BREAKFAST' (CENTER) 'CRIMSON CRUNCH' (RIGHT)

RADISHES

It wasn't love at first taste with radishes and me, but after a few years of growing them, they've become one of my favorite garden snacks to munch on as I meander about the beds. Radishes have a stellar reputation for being one of the easiest veggies to grow, and they can be. But they can also be a bit frustrating and fail to bulb (overcrowding and weather are often factors). Nonetheless, this is a terrific garden veggie, and its round, cheery charm is sure to capture a gardener's heart.

WHEN TO SOW
Direct sow as early as the soil can be worked.

SOIL
Sandy soil rich in potassium

PREFERRED LIGHT
Part shade to full sun

Tips + Tricks

GROWING

◆ Companion plant with peas, cucumbers, squash, spinach, carrots, and lettuce to boost both growth and flavor, as well as manage pests like cucumber beetles and squash borers. Avoid planting near brassicas.

◆ Get better germination by covering your planting area with black plastic for 4 to 5 days before sowing. While the key to happy radishes is to grow them in cool weather, the seeds need warmth in order to germinate. After your sowing area has warmed, pull back the plastic, sow the seeds, and re-cover with the plastic. After 3 to 4 days, peek under to look for germination. If you see sprouts, remove the plastic and let the seedlings grow.

◆ Use as row markers. Radishes are an easy and edible way to delineate sowings of vegetables like lettuce, carrots, and spinach.

◆ Toss with carrot seeds and grow together. Radishes help keep the soil aerated, which encourages carrot root growth.

◆ Sow a row or two every 2 weeks and you'll have radishes all season long. Best to skip sowing during the peak of summer, however, because radishes are more likely to bolt than bulb in heat.

STORING

◆ Place unwashed radishes in an airtight bag; should keep for 1 to 2 weeks.

◆ Store in a mason jar to maintain radishes' garden freshness at its best. Stem and wash the radishes, put them in the jar, fill the jar with water, and store in the refrigerator. Replace the water every other day.

EATING

◆ Eat those greens—they're full of vitamins and antioxidants. Toss young leaves in salads. Add mature leaves to soups and stews, sautés, and casseroles.

Favorite Varieties

'French Breakfast', 'Easter Egg', 'Cherriette', 'Cherry Belle'

EAT
RADISH SEEDPODS

Have you ever eaten a radish seedpod? Who knew that complete neglect could result in such a tasty delight? It's fabulous! I had a radish patch that I didn't realize had gone to flower until one of the pretty blossoms caught my eye. The flowers look a bit like phlox, so I let the rest of the patch bloom. A few weeks later, the flowers dropped and these plump seedpods appeared. Curious, I tasted one and was immediately hooked. It has the texture of a snap pea, with a mild radish bite—crisp happiness. I love them in salads and pickled, but they're also great in stir-fries or sautés. All varieties produce the seedpods, but if you still can't get enough, there is a variety called 'Rat's Tail' that is grown specifically for these delicious pods.

LETTUCE

Nothing beats sauntering out to the garden, empty bowl in hand, and returning with a heaping pile of lettuce of all different hues and textures. More than just a tasty veg to nosh on, lettuce makes a stunning garden border, especially when planted in a mix-and-match of different-colored and -textured varieties.

WHEN TO SOW
Direct sow as early as the soil can be worked; lettuce prefers cool climates. (Heat bitters the leaves.)

SOIL
Moist soil rich in nitrogen

PREFERRED LIGHT
Part sun

Tips + Tricks

◆ Pick leaves from the outside in to prolong the harvest of loose-leaf varieties, like 'Black Seeded Simpson' or 'Freckles'.

◆ Protect lettuce from summer's heat by growing it with tomato plants, which provide much-needed shade.

◆ Harvest in the morning, when lettuce's sugar content is at its highest.

◆ Get those greens in the refrigerator as soon as possible after harvesting; lettuce begins to wilt in as little as 15 minutes.

Companion plant with beets, carrots, radishes, onions, cucumbers, peas, tomatoes, and strawberries. Best to keep away from brassicas.

'BUTTERCRUNCH'

'GARNET ROSE'

Favorite Varieties

'Flashy Trout Back', 'Buttercrunch', 'Freckles', 'Black Seeded Simpson', 'Parris Island', 'Speckles', 'Red Sails', 'Garnet Rose'

'FLASHY TROUT BACK'

'GREEN SALAD BOWL'
'RED SALAD BOWL'

EAT

NO MORE WILTED LETTUCE

Here is the secret to storing your freshly harvested lettuce, so that the leaves stay crisp! Fill a salad spinner with cold water and soak the leaves, gently swishing them about to loosen any dirt. Lift the leaves out of the water and rinse again to remove any remaining grit. Spin the leaves to remove as much moisture as possible. Lay out a clean tea towel (or several paper towels) and arrange the leaves in a single layer across the towel. Gently roll up the towel and tuck it into a plastic bag, leaving the bag only loosely sealed so that some air can get in. The leaves will stay crisp and fresh for up to 10 days.

HERBAL VINAIGRETTES

These two vinaigrettes are in constant rotation in our home. Used as a salad dressing, a marinade, or even a happy drizzle over bruschetta or tuna, they make every meal tasty.

LEMON HERB DRESSING

- ½ cup extra-virgin olive oil
- ¼ cup lemon juice
- 2 tablespoons chopped chives
- 2 tablespoons chopped fresh parsley
- 2 teaspoons grated lemon zest
- 2 teaspoons honey
- 2 teaspoons Dijon mustard
- 2 teaspoons fresh tarragon

Combine ingredients in a jar and shake well. Season with salt and freshly ground black pepper. Store in the refrigerator for up to 5 days.

RED WINE VINAIGRETTE

- ⅓ cup extra-virgin olive oil
- 2 tablespoons red wine vinegar
- 1 teaspoon Dijon mustard
- 1 minced garlic clove

Whisk ingredients together and season with salt and freshly ground black pepper.

THYME

BASIL

OREGANO

Herbs: The Possibilities Are Endless

In my two decades of gardening, one group of plants has grown consistently and reliably for me: herbs. Along with their sheer beauty in the garden, these amazing, versatile plants offer such a diverse array of benefits that even after all these years, I still learn new uses for them.

Self-Sufficient Growers

One of the upsides of growing herbs is that they really don't need your help. You don't need to fertilize them, most pests leave them alone, and they rarely cry out for water. Other than being pinched back to promote bushiness and growth, they're fairly low maintenance. In addition, there are so many wonderful perennial and self-seeding annual herbs that, once established, take care of making new plants for you! Herbs grow beautifully in containers and don't mind soaking in the sun on an indoor windowsill.

Harvest More, Produce More

It's a brilliant thing: The more you harvest from your herbs, the more they'll produce (but please never harvest more than one-third of a plant at a time). If you plan to put your herbs to use in the kitchen, it's best not to let the plants go to flower; once they do, their leaves turn bitter. For peak flavor, harvest the leaves right before the flowers begin to form. This is when the herb's volatile oil content is highest, packing the most flavor into every leaf.

Enjoy Year-Round

One of my favorite parts of growing herbs is that they provide year-round enjoyment. In spring, you're busy sowing seed. Come summer, it's grow time, with daily harvests. Fall calls for bunching, gathering, and drying. And nothing takes the bite out of winter like spending time sifting, sorting, and jarring up beautiful, flavorful herbs.

GROW

COMPANION PLANT WITH HERBS

Aromatic herbs are a gardener's best companion plants. The volatile oils of some herbs act as a repellant to many insect pests: Rosemary, sage, and parsley all help deter nasty carrot flies, while calendula and borage keep tomato hornworms at bay. While some herbs lend a hand in pest control, others boost the growth and flavor of veggies. Carrots are tastier and grow better when sown with chives. Of course, let's not forget the love affair that is tomatoes and basil. Remember: For the most part, herbs and veggies that partner well together in the kitchen also grow well together in the garden.

USE THOSE BLOOMS

When you deadhead your favorite garden blooms, like calendulas and violas, the plants will blossom longer, putting out seemingly endless flowers. Rather than toss these plucked pretties into the compost, you can create hanging displays, dry them to use in herbal skin-care products, preserve them by pressing them in books, or make art prints by lightly hammering the flowers on paper.

CHIVES

Chives' endearing qualities will sneak up on you! The edible flowers make an enchanting pink-hued vinegar—one of the first herb preserves of the growing season. The endless charm of its beckoning blooms produce a nonstop hustle and bustle of pollinators, yet the odor of the plant will deter deer. Chive blossoms also keep their pretty lilac hue when dried, making them perfect for everlasting flower arrangements.

WHEN TO SOW
Direct sow in early spring as soon as the soil can be worked; plants take a year or so to become established.

SOIL
Compost-rich, moist soil

PREFERRED LIGHT
Full sun to part shade

LEEK BLOSSOMS

Tips + Tricks

◆ Companion plant with carrots, celery, squash, peppers, tomatoes, and roses. Chives' aroma deters pests like aphids, cabbageworms, Japanese beetles, slugs, and cucumber beetles. Keep them away from peas and beans.

◆ Start seeds indoors 6 to 8 weeks before the last frost date.

◆ Keep new plants well watered throughout their first season. Once established, plants can withstand drier conditions.

◆ Create more plants by dividing clumps every 3 years.

◆ Deadhead to avoid spread. Chives self-sow with abandon! Each chive blossom is made up of hundreds of tiny florets—and each of those will bear a seed. So if you don't cut back the plant before it sets seed, you may wake to a chive invasion next spring.

◆ Use chives to attract pollinators and boost pollination rates of neighboring plants. This is one of the most pollinator-friendly plants in my garden. The flowers are always abuzz with activity from beneficial insects, butterflies, and bees.

Favorite Varieties

Aside from the standard garden chives, there are a few other varieties of chives and alliums to try if you find yourself hooked on nibbling those blossoms. Incorporate garlic chives into the mix for a flourish of white pom-pom flowers. Let some onions, garlic, and leeks over-winter, and you'll reap the rewards of their showstopping blooms the following summer. Leek blossoms are particularly stunning; each plant shoots up a 5-foot-tall stalk capped with a globe of teeny white star-shaped flowers. I find them so gorgeous that I'm not sure anymore if I'm growing leeks for eating or for gazing at.

GARLIC CHIVES

GROW

Cut and Come Again

Chives are a cut-and-come-again herb, meaning the more you use, the more the plant will produce. If kept clipped, the plant will continuously produce new foliage. On the flipside, though, keeping it clipped means that it won't set those delicious purple blossoms. I tend to keep half my plants clipped back and let the other half go to flower.

If not clipped back, chive stems become woody over time. And once allowed to flower, the herb will focus on setting seed rather than developing new growth. I cut back all my flowering chives to 2 inches above the ground after the last flower has been picked. By doing this, fresh growth will pop up, and I'll get a second crop of fresh chives perfectly timed for late-summer noshing.

CHIVE BLOSSOM VINEGAR

One of my favorite garden treats, this zesty vinegar not only adds a mild onion flavor to everything from salads to stir-fries, but also bottles up to one of the prettiest hues of pink you've ever seen. Wash and gently pat dry a handful of fresh chive blossoms. Fill a sterilized mason jar two-thirds of the way with blossoms. Pour distilled white vinegar over them, filling to the top of the jar. Using a wooden spoon, gently crush the blossoms. Cap with a plastic or other nonreactive lid and place the jar in a cool, dark spot for at least 2 weeks. Give the jar a good shake each day. Strain through cheesecloth into a sterile bottle and enjoy. Use within 6 months to 1 year for the best flavor.

MORE CHIVE NIBBLES

✳ Gently break apart the flower clusters into individual florets and sprinkle them for a subtle, savory, oniony addition to salads, risottos, burgers, and tuna fish sandwiches.

✳ The flowers' subtle flavor takes on a deep, oniony bite when dried. Grind dried flowers into a powder and add to grilling rubs, salts, and salad dressings.

✳ Dried chive leaves don't maintain their taste and loveliness; instead, chop them while fresh, then either place them in a plastic bag and freeze or put them in an ice cube tray, cover them with olive oil, and store in the freezer.

SPRING

39

LEMON BALM

If you have lemon balm in your garden, chances are you have a lot of it. This perennial herb is a member of the mint family and loves to self-sow little legacies everywhere. To help control it, give the plant a good haircut to prevent it from flowering and setting seed. This also preserves the tastiness of the leaves and keeps the plants bushy and fat.

WHEN TO SOW
Start indoors 6 to 8 weeks before the last frost date.

SOIL
Moist, compost-rich, well-drained soil

PREFERRED LIGHT
Full sun; tolerates part shade

Fresh Is Best

❋ This balm's lemony goodness is best consumed fresh.

❋ To keep some of that fresh flavor on hand even in winter, chop some leaves and place in ice cube trays, then cover with vegetable oil and freeze. Pop a cube or two into baked goods or vinaigrettes for a garden-fresh lemony kick.

❋ Pour yourself a crisp, zesty cup of tea to go with lemon balm shortbread or pound cake.

❋ Use lemon balm in place of lemon peel to flavor soups, sauces, and vinegars.

❋ Toss into a salad or mix with fresh fruit.

Tips + Tricks

◆ Companion plant with broccoli, cabbage, and kale. Turns out, all those horrible pests that prey on your brassicas do not like the bright citrus scent of lemon balm.

◆ Seeds are very slow to germinate and will require light to do so; avoid covering them with growing medium.

◆ Avoid fertilizing, as that diminishes lemon balm's lovely scent.

◆ Avoid growing in humid, hot zones, as this herb prefers cooler growing conditions.

◆ Plant it near any crop you want to draw pollinators to. Lemon balm's very appropriate genus name, *Melissa*, means "honeybee" in Greek. Bees will flock by the dozens to sip on its sweet nectar.

◆ Add dried lemon balm leaves to potpourri, sachets, and sleep pillows.

SUN TEA

Nothing refreshes on a hot summer day quite like a cup of lemon balm sun tea. It not only boosts the mood but warms the soul.

You can brew up a batch of this as you hang out in the garden. Simply place 1 to 2 cups fresh lemon balm (or mix it up with your favorite herbs) in a 1-quart mason jar. Pour 1 quart water over the herbs and let the jar sit in the sun all day. Strain and enjoy the tea over ice. Refrigerate any leftovers for up to 3 days.

CHAMOMILE

Chamomile will quickly spread its garden cheer with a profusion of flowers just 60 days from germination.

WHEN TO SOW
Sow indoors 6 weeks before your last frost date.

SOIL
Well-drained soil

PREFERRED LIGHT
Full sun

Tips + Tricks

GROWING

◆ Don't start seedlings too early. Larger seedlings don't transplant as well as younger ones. Rather, set seedlings out in the garden once they've grown their first three or four true leaves.

HARVESTING & USING

◆ Pick chamomile flowers in the morning when they are fully open but after the dew has dried.

◆ Dry flower heads on a screen, or on newspaper placed on a rack, for good airflow.

◆ Give your drying chamomile a daily gentle shake to ensure even drying.

◆ When the flowers crumble to the touch, they're dry and ready to be stored in a nonporous container, away from heat and light.

◆ Use the flowers fresh or dried in tea.

Medicinal Properties

Antispasmodic, anti-inflammatory, antimicrobial, antioxidant, analgesic

Types: German or Roman

German and Roman chamomile are different plant species that offer similar herbal properties. German chamomile (*Matricaria recutita*) is an annual that grows best in Zones 4 to 9; it may not flourish in regions with hot summers. It grows up to 2 feet tall and has a sweeter taste. Roman chamomile (*Chamaemelum nobile*) is a low-growing perennial hardy to Zones 4 to 9 that spreads via rhizomes, making it a heaven-scented ground cover.

NOURISH

Herbal Hair Rinse

Achieve healthy locks by cleansing and boosting circulation to your scalp and conditioning your hair with this nourishing rinse. Pour 2 cups boiling water over ¼ cup fresh or dried chamomile flowers. Let the mixture cool, then strain out all the solids and use. This rinse is best for lighter hair. If you have brown hair, use sage rather than chamomile.

TOSS & GO
A Win for Lazy
Gardening

Harvesting chamomile is backbreaking work. So when I mistakenly yank up a chamomile plant, I'll admit to mindlessly tossing it in the air and letting it fall where it may, rather than trekking to the compost pile or the chicken coop to dispose of it.

Turns out, I nurture my neighboring plants by taking the lazy approach. In fact, brassicas, onions, cucumbers, and beans all benefit from a good sprinkling of chamomile clippings around their roots. These clippings add calcium, magnesium, and potassium to the soil, giving nearby plants a nutrient boost.

·······································

CHAMOMILE PATHWAYS

My success with growing lots of chamomile resides in pretty much removing myself from the whole process and just letting Mother Nature do her thing. I used to try to contain my chamomile in nice, neat areas, but the plants' tendency to self-sow was stronger than my ability to remove them from their newfound homes. That and the fact that these strapping, vibrant volunteer chamomiles put my own seed-sown ones to shame. So now, each spring, I allow the chamomile to run amok across the pathways. By doing so, I minimize the need for weeding, give a boost to neighboring plants, and best of all . . . I gather nonstop chamomile harvests for 2 solid months.

When the end of July rolls around and the plants begin to look scraggly and run down, I'll reclaim the pathways by clearing out the chamomile in one big swath. Clearing them away helps manage the number of seeds that drop. I already have chamomile pathways everywhere—I don't need a *forest* of it! (Though that does sound quite lovely.)

 NOURISH

Serenity Now: Mindful Tea in the Garden

Are your shoulders practically touching your ears? Let chamomile chase away tension and stress with every sip, soak, and scent. For hundreds of years, chamomile has been known to calm and soothe. Double up on the relaxation by enjoying that cup of tea while you soak in a chamomile-infused bath: Chamomile's anti-inflammatory and antispasmodic (calms muscle cramps and spasms) properties aid in quieting aches and cramps as the tea relaxes your nervous system. The tea is also great for stomachaches and digestive issues. Infuse some chamomile in oil and use it to soothe wounds and rashes, or make chamomile ice cubes and gently glide them over inflamed skin. Chamomile loves to help your skin be happy and healthy.

Note: If you have a ragweed allergy, it's best to avoid chamomile.

BREW A PERFECT CUP OF CHAMOMILE

As a professed tea oversteeper (more like tea *forgetter*), I often brew a cup, only to remember it 30 minutes later. But that would be a shame to do with chamomile, because if you let it steep too long, it becomes bitter. Plus you want to capture all the goodness of chamomile's volatile oils. So steep for just 3 to 5 minutes, keeping a tight lid on your mug to trap in those oils. Remove the cover and breathe in the steam. Then sit back, sip, and relax away the cares of the day.

Violas pack plenty of blooms in a petite package. Perfect for front borders, they grow 6 to 8 inches tall and produce flowers 12 to 14 weeks from sowing.

VIOLA

These cool-weather-loving, short-lived perennials with sweet, slightly fragrant blooms go by many names: heartsease, tricolor violas, wild pansies, and johnny jump ups. Whatever name you choose is all good, as long as you include this timeless, charming beauty in your garden.

WHEN TO SOW
Start indoors 8 to 10 weeks before transplanting outside 4 weeks before the last frost date; direct sow 4 to 6 weeks before the last frost date.

SOIL
Average

PREFERRED LIGHT
Full morning sun and afternoon shade

Tips + Tricks

◆ Get better germination by covering the seeds completely when sowing; violas need darkness to germinate.

◆ Deadhead frequently for nonstop blooms from spring to frost—and to keep the plants from self-seeding too widely. Give plants a good chop during the hottest parts of summer to keep them from getting leggy.

◆ Create a stunning display that will beckon bees by grouping a cluster of different-size containers. Keep the plants within arm's reach for easy picking; you can freeze their edible flowers into ice cubes or toss them onto salads.

Medicinal Properties

Antimicrobial, anti-inflammatory, antioxidant, antiseptic

More than a Pretty Face

These delicate little floral faces gently soothe skin and help to reduce redness, calm skin irritations like eczema and acne, quench dry skin, take the sting out of insect bites, and crush cradle cap. Violas are wonderful in infused oils, poultices, and salves, or you can brew up this infusion for a quick skin soother:

Place a handful of violas in a cup. Pour boiling water over the flowers. Cover the cup and let steep for 15 minutes. Remove the cover and breathe in the herbal steam, rich with viola's volatile oils. Once the infusion has cooled, apply to the skin using a cotton towel or pad.

SPRING FLORAL DUSTING POWDER

Violas offer cooling, soothing properties for your skin. As summer's heat and humidity build, what better thing to make with these blossoms than a refreshing floral dusting powder that blots up excess moisture and odors, keeping you feeling fresh as a, well, viola?

- ⅔ cup dried violas
- ⅔ cup dried peppermint
- ½ cup arrowroot powder or cornstarch
- ½ cup kaolin clay

Place the violas and peppermint in a coffee grinder (ideally, not the one you actually grind coffee in). Alternatively, if you're up for building some arm muscles, use a mortar and pestle. Grind the herbs into a fine powder. Transfer the powdered herbs to a bowl and mix with the arrowroot and kaolin. Break up any lumps. For the smoothest texture, sift the mixture through a fine-mesh strainer. Pour the powder into a shaker bottle and sprinkle away.

SWEET VIOLA TUB SOAK

Violas are known to aid in reducing stress and anxiety. Dive into spring with this sweet floral soak.

- ½ cup Epsom salts or sea salt
- ¼ cup viola or pansy petals
- 2 tablespoons extra-coarse sea salt
- 1 tablespoon sea salt
- 1 ounce baking soda
- 4 drops essential oil of choice (optional)

Combine the Epsom salts and flower petals in a mini food processor. Blend until the flowers are completely incorporated. Spread the salt mixture in a thin layer on a sheet of wax paper and let air-dry for 1 to 2 days.

Once it has air-dried, crumble the dried floral salt into a bowl and stir in the sea salt and baking soda. You can leave the soak unscented or mix in the essential oil now, if desired.

TO USE: Pour the mixture into a bathtub while it fills with comfortably warm water. Alternatively, to make cleanup easy and keep petal fragments out of your drain, tie up the mixture in a muslin tea bag or a clean sock before adding it to the tub.

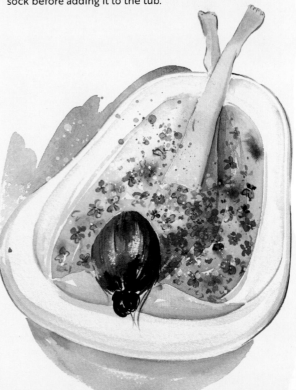

CORNFLOWERS

When I first started growing cornflowers, also known as bachelor's buttons, I was more of a gardener than an herbalist. I credit this charming blue blossom—abounding with anti-inflammatory and antioxidant qualities—for taking my study of herbs out of the kitchen . . . and into a whole new world.

WHEN TO SOW
Direct sow in spring 2 weeks
before the last frost date.
(Cornflowers do not transplant well.)

SOIL
Moist, well-drained soil

PREFERRED LIGHT
Full sun; may flop with
insufficient sun

48

Tips + Tricks

- Chill the seeds in the refrigerator for 1 week prior to sowing to improve germination.
- Deadhead regularly for continued blooms.
- Plant in large groupings to attract hoverflies. These beneficial insects are not only powerful pollinators but are also predators of aphids and thrips.
- Plant in partnership with calendula, poppies, and larkspur for a gorgeous combination.

USING

- Add a dazzle of blue to your dishes, along with a clovelike bite, as cornflower's petals make wonderful edible flowers.
- Dry the flowers to enjoy through winter and use to craft your own skin-care products.
- Make a beautiful blue dye by boiling the petals in water with a mordant, like alum.

Cornflowers aren't truly blue; plants have no way of making blue pigment. In fact, it's a bit of botanical magic that modifies the flower's red pigments by shifting their pH balance.

NOURISH

Cornflowers for Your Skin

There are all kinds of ways cornflower is good for the skin. Its cooling and toning properties help diminish fine lines and wrinkles around the eyes, firm and brighten skin, and reduce puffiness. Its anti-inflammatory properties calm acne-prone skin and soothe sensitive skin, especially when combined with chamomile. Infuse flowers in rose hip or sweet almond oil and apply to the skin daily.

MAKE YOUR OWN HERBAL FACIAL STEAM

Treat yourself to a relaxing and rejuvenating facial steam, using cornflowers alone or combining them with other favorite herbs. Begin with a clean face. Heat enough hot water to fill a wide bowl. Place the herbs in the bowl and slowly pour the hot water over them. Seat yourself comfortably, lean over the bowl, and cover your head and the bowl with a towel, trapping the soothing steam. For 8 to 10 minutes, sit, relax, and breathe in the herbs' volatile oils. When done, splash your face with cool water and gently pat dry. Finish by massaging your face with a few drops of your favorite herb-infused oil. Now go out and glow.

POPPIES

Poppies are no wallflower. Their captivating colors on silken petals shine like beacons across the garden. Their majestic flowers immediately entrance. And the bumbles these blooms attract are unparalleled. Plant Papaver somniferum varieties, like 'Hungarian Breadseed', and you'll be greeted with a sea of stunning volunteers for many years to come.

WHEN TO SOW
Direct sow in early spring as soon as the soil can be worked.

SOIL
Well-drained soil

PREFERRED LIGHT
Full sun

Tips + Tricks

GROWING

- Lightly cover the seeds after sowing.
- Start seeds in winter outdoors in milk jugs. (See page 196.)
- Deadhead spent blooms to extend flowering.
- Cut back the plants after the first flush of blooms, and the plant may produce a second round of flowers later in the season.
- Propagate Oriental poppies from root cuttings rather than seeds. These poppies are hybrids, which won't produce a true-to-parent plant when grown from seed.

EATING

- Take your baked goods to the next level with homegrown poppy seeds. Look for breadseed varieties.

'HUNGARIAN BREADSEED'

ORIENTAL POPPY

SEED PODS

'HUNGARIAN BREADSEED'

ORIENTAL POPPY

PHLOX

Pollinators of all sorts will flock to phlox. It's a favorite of butterflies, along with myriad moths.

WHEN TO SOW
Sow indoors 4 weeks before the last frost date.

SOIL
Well-drained, compost-rich soil

PREFERRED LIGHT
Full sun; tolerates light shade

Tips + Tricks

◆ Choose which phlox works best for you. Phlox is available in perennial and annual varieties that range in height from ground cover to 5 feet tall.

◆ Brighten up partly shady spots by planting the ground-cover and dwarf varieties.

◆ Avoid growing if you live in a drought-prone area, as phlox requires continuous moisture to flourish. Mulch to help retain moisture.

◆ Create a striking grouping in your garden by growing tall phlox in combination with 'Queeny Lime Orange' zinnias and anise hyssop, or pair with rudbeckia and bee balm.

GARDEN PHLOX

'ROYAL CARPET'

'PASTEL BLEND'

SWEET ALYSSUM

You grow garden happiness when you incorporate borders of sweet alyssum into your landscape. From early spring through first frost, you'll be greeted by bountiful low bushes of tiny, honey-scented blossoms that beckon bees from all around. It's especially rewarding to start from seed, since its first blooms emerge as early as 6 weeks after germination.

WHEN TO SOW	SOIL	PREFERRED LIGHT
Start indoors 4 to 6 weeks before the last frost date.	Compost-rich, well-drained soil	Full sun; tolerates partial shade

Tips + Tricks

◆ Sweet alyssum needs light to germinate. Help ensure good germination by not covering the seeds when sowing. Rather, gently press the seeds into the top of the soil to help anchor them.

◆ Sow a few seeds together in clusters, rather than one seed per cell, and transplant the cluster into the garden after the last frost date.

◆ Stop to smell the honey-scented blossoms. These strongly fragrant flowers help repel pests and attract beneficial insects like lacewings and parasitic wasps.

◆ Create stunning front-border displays by sowing sweet alyssum in large groupings, which also help keep down weeds. As an extra benefit, this flower acts as a natural mulch when planted under larger plants.

SWEET PEAS

Did you know that not all sweet peas are scented? Grandiflora varieties are best known for their delicious scent. Grow 'Cupani', 'Matucana', and 'Painted Lady' to delight in their intoxicating fragrance.

WHEN TO SOW Direct sow in early spring as soon as the soil can be worked, or start indoors 4 to 6 weeks before the last frost date.

SOIL Well-drained, rich soil amended with lots of compost

PREFERRED LIGHT Full sun

Tips + Tricks

◆ Soak the seeds in water for 24 hours before sowing to hasten germination.

◆ Be sure to cover the seeds completely when sowing; sweet peas need darkness to germinate.

◆ Sow in deep pots so sweet peas' long roots have room to stretch out. I sow four seeds to a 4-inch pot, then thin out the weakest seedling, leaving three seedlings in the pot.

◆ Pinch back for bushiness and more sumptuously scented blooms. When the seedlings are 6 inches tall, pinch the tops to promote branching. Be sure to leave three or four leaf nodules on the plant.

◆ Plant a border of low-growing beauties like sweet alyssum, petunias, violas, or lobelia around sweet peas' base to help keep the soil cool, which they prefer.

◆ Keep well watered, as they will not thrive in dry conditions.

◆ Avoid fertilizing early in the season, as that promotes leaf growth at the expense of flower production. Instead, plant in compost-rich soil to provide the right amount of nutrients until flowering.

◆ Feed with a high-potassium fertilizer when blossoms appear.

◆ Gather the flowers in the cool of the morning, when still damp with dew. This is when their scent is the sweetest.

◆ Pick the flowers frequently to encourage continued blooming.

SNAPDRAGONS

My favorite bee and bloom memory is of witnessing a quiet stem of snapdragons come alive and begin to sway. Then suddenly, a flower unhinged its jaw-of-sorts, and a happy bumblebee wiggled its way out, back end first. I've never just walked past a cluster of snapdragons since. Rather, I meander for a bit, hoping to catch another bee-utiful moment.

WHEN TO SOW
Start indoors 8 to 10 weeks
before the last frost date.

SOIL Compost-rich,
well-drained soil

PREFERRED LIGHT
Full sun to part shade

Tips + Tricks

- Cover the seeds very lightly with vermiculite when sowing, as the seeds need light to germinate. Transplant into the garden after the last frost date.

- Create bushier plants brimming with more blooms by pinching back the seedlings when they are 4 to 6 inches tall. This encourages branching.

- Cut back after the first flush of flowers. This keeps the plant from setting seed and encourages the development of a second flush of pollinator-beckoning blooms.

- Prolong flowering by feeding with a potassium-rich fertilizer and pinching off spent flowers and seedpods.

- Plant pink snapdragons, trailing amaranth, and 'Opus' asters for a stunning combination.

BORAGE

NASTURTIUM

VIOLET

LAVENDER

Edible Flowers:
Love at First Bite

My love affair with edible and medicinal flowers began a long time ago when I caught on to the fact that the more I deadheaded these blooms, the longer they lasted, putting out seemingly endless flowers. It felt like such a shame to toss these plucked pretties into the compost, so I began to research how to use them and, in doing so, opened a whole new world. Today, I use these harvests for everything from decorating our tables to garnishing salads to slathering on my skin—and so much more!

NASTURTIUM

SQUASH

VIOLAS

CHIVES

EAT

What Do They Taste Like?

Truth be told, except for strong floral herbs like lavender and rose, the overall taste of edible flowers is subtle, but their impact is pretty large. A small handful of edible flowers tossed in a salad or sprinkled over pasta can brighten up your meal.

Anise
licorice-like

Bee balm
hint of mint

Borage
crisp cucumber

Calendula
slightly bitter, with a mild, peppery bite

Chamomile
sweet with apple aroma

Chives
mild onion overtones

Cornflower
slightly clovelike

Dahlias
flavor varies with each variety

Dandelions
sweet, honeylike when picked young

Daylilies
sweet with a note of squash

Dill flowers
milder dill taste

Hibiscus
bit of a citrus zing

Honeysuckle
sweet nectar

Lavender
strong floral notes

Nasturtiums
peppery, like watercress

Pansies
greens/grassy

Pea blossoms
milder pea taste

Red clover
licorice-like

Roses
sweet floral

Squash blossoms
hint of nectar taste

Sweet alyssum
sweet peppery notes

Violas
hint of mint

Violet
subtle, sweet floral

LET THEM BLOOM

Enjoy your herbs and their flowers, too! Letting culinary herbs like oregano, sage, and thyme go to flower means you can enjoy their tasty blossoms. Once your culinary herbs bloom, though, their leaves will become bitter as the plant focuses more on flower and seed production than on growing foliage. So plant an extra pot or two of herbs you'll let flower—for both your snacks and your pollinator pals—and cut back the rest.

THE ART OF EDIBLE FLOWERS

Add personality and allure to drinks and dishes by incorporating edible flowers from your garden. Freeze a few flowers in ice cube trays and transform any drink instantly. Sprinkle flowers onto salads for a dazzling effect. Even bake them into your next tray of cookies and astound everyone with their charm.

There are many more options out there in your garden. Borage blossoms offer a crisp cucumber-like bite. Nasturtiums and day-lilies add a peppery kick to salads. Lavender's floral notes brighten up baked goods, while bee balm brings a minty taste. And of course, big, bright, beautiful squash blossoms can be stuffed, baked, fried . . . you name it.

So put that vase aside and grab a fork! Enjoying edible florals is as easy as popping off a blossom (cleaned and washed, of course!) and tossing it on.

Harvesting Edible Flowers

Harvest only the most vibrant, healthy blossoms.

. . . .

Edible flowers are best eaten the day they are picked (though they can last in the refrigerator for a few days).

. . . .

Harvest in the early morning, right after the dew has dried but before the sun beats down.

. . . .

Gently wash and dry before using.

. . . .

Eat only flowers that have not been sprayed with pesticides (though hopefully you are growing organically!).

Caution: For safety's sake, make sure to clearly identify a plant before eating it. If there is any doubt, do not consume.

EDIBLE FLOWERS & HERB COMPOUND BUTTER

Transform a simple stick of butter into a celebration of herbs and edible flowers! I like to use whatever fresh herbs I have on hand, including rosemary, oregano, thyme, sage, scallions, and calendula. Soften a stick of unsalted butter in a medium bowl. Finely chop a handful of your favorite herbs and fold them into the softened butter. Line a container or mold with plastic wrap, fill it with the compound butter, and refrigerate until the butter is set, 1 to 2 hours. If desired, you can decorate the set butter with additional herbs and edible flowers. Keep in the refrigerator for up to 1 week or freeze for up to 3 months.

BEE BALM

COLEUS

COLUMBINE

BLEEDING HEART

PANSY

FERNS AND FORGET-ME-NOT

GOOD PLANTS
for the Shade

Plants that are fans of shade tend to prefer cool, moist weather. They also don't mind getting less than 6 hours of sun a day. Plants that are grown for their foliage tend to tolerate even less sun, but those that flower will like to bask in the sun's rays for at least a few hours a day.

Here are a few favorites for low-light landscapes.

Astilbe

Bee balm

Begonia

Bleeding heart

Coleus

Columbine

Ferns

Forget-me-not

Hellebore

Hosta

Impatiens

Leopard plant

Lily of the valley

Pansies

Primrose

Snapdragon

Sweet Annie

Sweet woodruff

Virginia bluebell

Wood anemone

Grow Your Own Birdseed

My bird pals are some of my best garden helpers. Their noshing on flower seed heads not only drops seeds below, creating volunteer plants galore, but they also carry some of those seeds to different corners of the garden, gifting it with patches of anise hyssop, echinacea, and rudbeckia. By sowing these seeds now, you'll provide a valuable food source for migrating and resident birds come autumn and winter. The seed heads are nutritional powerhouses just when your feathered friends need them the most.

Here are a few favorite seed heads to grow for your bird pals.

Anise hyssop

Aster

Echinacea

Evening primrose

Mullein

Ornamental grasses

Rudbeckia

Sunflower

Zinnia

Provide a Water Source for Birds

Having a source of fresh water for your feathered and winged friends is always important, especially during unexpected heat waves when not a drop of rain is to be had. It's easy to make your own watering station. Choose a setup that you can easily clean every week. Consistency is also key; if you are consistent with providing fresh water, birds will consistently visit.

I use galvanized tubs for my waterers, which I fill with several large rocks—including a few that jut above the waterline to provide an island respite—and place in a sheltered location that offers shade. My main tub is right on the garden's edge, close to what I call the Hemlock Hotel, a favorite haunt of my garden's birds. They quickly swoop in and out for a drink, sometimes staying longer to freshen up with a bath. I provide fresh water each day. Once a week, I scrub the tub and rocks.

Foraging from Nature's Spring Garden

My first harvests of spring often don't come from my garden; rather, they come from pockets and nooks throughout my woods, supplemented with scores found when visiting favorite local foraging haunts. There's something soul soothing about heading out into the wild with just a basket and shears in hand and returning with a bounty of nature's treasures. Foraging is a wonderful way to connect with the natural world, but it comes with a certain amount of responsibility as well: to take only a little and to leave a whole lot. Proper harvesting sustains the plant, and thus sustains the foraging community.

As lovely as the flowers are, the lion's share of violet's nutrients resides in the leaves, including vitamins A and C and calcium.

Tips for Safe Foraging

✻ Only forage from properties where you have permission to collect.

✻ Minimize your impact on the property.

✻ Make sure the area is pesticide free.

✻ Make sure the area is at least 50 feet away from busy roadsides.

✻ Wash collected plants before using.

Violets

As soon as the snow melts and the first sprigs of green pop up, you can find me meandering about, basket in hand, collecting nips of nettles and handfuls of dandelion leaves, fiddleheads, ramps, and my favorite: wild violets. Since childhood, I have adored these charming flowers. While some may consider violets to be a bit of a weed, they're actually little herbal powerhouses. Nutrient-rich, violets are chock-full of vitamins A and C and calcium. So start noshing on those flowers and leaves! Sprinkle some on your salads, or sugar them and use them to decorate desserts. Why not infuse honey with them (a spoonful soothes coughs and sore throats)? Or what about crafting a batch of violet vinegar or syrup? Personally, my favorite is simply to freeze the blossoms into ice cube trays and dazzle guests with flower-filled cocktails.

VIOLET SUGAR

pH Litmus Test

One of the cool things about violets is that they can act as a pH test of sorts. The composition of the plant makes it a perfect base, in solution, to test the effects of an acidic element like lemon. Pure violet water is blue, but if you want it to be purple, you add a few drops of lemon juice and voilà, it changes hue. You can add a few drops more and it will change again, this time to pink. But note that all these drops of lemon juice will also take away from the delicate violet notes.

 EAT
VIOLET SYRUP

Refreshing and tasty in cocktails, iced teas, glazes, and frozen treats, this simple syrup is super simple to make. Combine 1 cup water and 1 cup sugar in a medium saucepan and boil until the sugar has dissolved. Remove from the heat, stir in 1 cup violet flowers and steep until cool. Strain and discard the solids, bottle the syrup, and keep refrigerated for up to 2 weeks.

 NOURISH
VIOLET SKIN SOOTHER

Medicinally speaking, violets offer incredible antimicrobial, anti-inflammatory, and soothing properties. They are wonderful in infused oils, poultices, and salves for dry skin, insect bites, cradle cap, and eczema. For a quick skin soother, steep 1 heaping tablespoon violets in 1 cup boiling water and allow to stand for 15 minutes. Strain out the flowers, cool the infusion, and apply it to irritated skin.

SPRING

63

Cultivating Wildness:
Pruning Wild Berries

"Cultivating wildness" is an oxymoron of sorts, but that's what I've been doing with our wild raspberries and blackberries for the past 15 years. Early each spring, when I'm still able to wear a good, thick winter coat and pants (for both warmth and thorn protection), I head out to our wild, brambling hedge along the wood's edge and prune out all the old, dark brown canes. Then I lop a good 10 inches off the tops of green canes. After consistently doing this for several years, our bounty of berries has increased in both yield and berry size.

I also trellis the raspberries along a bamboo fence, then gather the blackberry canes into tripods, tying the canes together at the top. Doing so not only makes picking a lot easier and less painful, but it ensures good airflow through the plants, helping to keep pesky diseases at bay.

KEEP DOMESTIC BERRIES AWAY FROM WILD ONES

Did you know you should always plant cultivated berries away from wild ones? Some wild berries carry viral diseases that can quickly take down your cultivated crops. So restrict the two to opposite areas of your garden, if possible!

64

Explore & Experiment

Even if it's just one small pot, have a little fun each season and try your hand at growing something completely new. Try veggies you've never heard of before, like cucamelons—a grape-size cucumber snack that I now grow every year. Or test your zone boundaries with plants that may not be the best fit for your area. I'm trying to grow ginger in the Maine woods!

Have fun, but take it as just that, because chances are these crops are more like garden gambles—with luck, they will grow and thrive, but they don't, it's still exciting to try something new and different. And you never know what may surprise you.

CUCAMELON

Some seed companies label Job's tears as being edible, but the variety of seed sold in North America has a rock-hard, inedible shell. The variety grown in Asia, known as Chinese barley, has a soft shell and can be eaten.

MAKE

Grow Your Own Jewelry

Job's tears grows like a corn-stalk (without the cob) and bears a grain that can be used as an ornamental bead. Over the course of one season on just four plants, I grew 150 beads, enough to make a few bracelets and a necklace. Once the grain dries, remove the husk from the bead and clean out the hollow, and you've got yourself a bead ready for stringing. The coolest part is that once dried, they have the same feel, weight, and sound (when clanked together) as glass beads.

Summer

A Time to Do

Summer brings with it a sensory explosion. Plants of different hues, in all different shapes and sizes take over the landscape. Aromatics explode as your hand tickles leaves as you pass. All around, a chorus of songbirds sends out joy with each note. And the tastes . . . where do I even begin? Each vegetable brings a taste bud treat whose subtle notes and sweetness beg to be eaten.

Summer is also a seemingly endless sprint of to-dos. Every free moment is a balancing act of growing, weeding, watering, and harvesting. You can easily become a victim of your own success and find yourself spending endless hours in the kitchen preserving that magnificent bounty. Today, I grow less for preserving and more for savoring throughout the growing season, and I use that freed-up time for sitting and basking in the garden. Harvests for the soul are more of what I grow these days.

The secret to true garden success is letting go and allowing Mother Nature to take the wheel. That's when the magic happens.

Grow with the Flow

With summer comes the fruition of all those garden plans you dreamed up in winter and all those seeds you sowed in spring. Looking around at summer's bounty absolutely feels like winning the lottery, but it can also be completely overwhelming, especially when you realize the time and effort needed not only to grow but to preserve that food.

Summer also brings the lion's share of pests and diseases. And depending on the weather, watering and weeding could easily be daily necessities. In essence, gardening in summer is a constant juggling act, and sometimes you need to choose how many balls you really want to keep in the air.

Gardening should be enjoyable. But we often forget that. For most of us, our reality is that, if push comes to shove, we can head to the market and pick up the ingredients for tonight's dinner. So we gardeners really shouldn't fret as much as we do. But we fret because we care. We love. We nurture. And then we get crushed when, regardless of all of that exertion, we fail. Before we know it, this so-called peaceful hobby of ours now grows a healthy crop of stress and worry with every carrot and tomato planted.

I spent way too many years gardening this way. Working so hard. Trying to "control" pests and diseases. Spending every minute in the garden, weeding, harvesting, planting. Being *productive*—or so I thought. I had great harvests over these years because of all that effort, but I was also very, very tired. I was working full-time, raising children, tending to animals. And then there were those dishes that always needed to be done. The time for much of my gardening came in what I call "stolen moments." And for most of my gardening life, I spent all those stolen moments working.

Until one fateful day almost a decade ago. Only a few weeks into the growing season, I lost a quarter of my garden to cabbage-root maggots. Every single strapping, healthy, hulking seedling in the brassica family was lost to a previously unknown soil demon whose presence was beyond my control. It was at that moment when it all just stopped: The worry. The fret. The anxiety. It was all gone. In its place came acceptance of the situation, acknowledgment of what I can and can't control, and I adopted a new mindset of gardening zen that I call "grow with the flow."

I'll admit to initially expecting this laid-back outlook to disappear as quickly as it came, but here we are, all these years later, and that feeling of garden peace has only grown deeper. And my garden has never looked more beautiful or been more full of life and harvests. And best of all, I am working less and enjoying so much more.

Turns out, the secret to true garden success is in letting go and allowing Mother Nature to take the wheel. That's when the magic happens, and your garden transforms into a paradise full of not only vegetables, herbs, and flowers but also a whole world of wildlife, pollinators, and visitors of all sorts. It truly becomes a wonderland.

Growing a Balanced Garden

I gardened for many years before I made a concentrated effort to introduce more flowers into my garden. At first, I was reluctant to share my valuable growing space with something my family couldn't eat. But the transformation the flowers brought was undeniable: The more flowers we had, the more pollinators we attracted, which led to the production of more produce.

Because I was already practicing companion planting—pairing vegetables in beneficial garden combinations—the natural next step was to introduce flowers and herbs to the veggie beds. Rather subconsciously, I created a garden that was equal thirds herbs, vegetables, and flowers. This combination created a balance in the garden so that, before long, it needed less and less of my assistance to battle the cucumber beetles, aphids, and stinkbugs, because armies of beneficial insects were taking on the fight. While the beneficial insects helped keep the pests at bay, the proliferation of pollinators that poured in had the garden buzzing with activity from spring through frost. The pollinators boosted not only the bushels of harvests but the bounty of blooms as well.

Meander Mindfully & Involve All the Senses

Garden bewilderment. Ever find yourself making a beeline for the garden, armed with a mental list of to-dos that you're determined to accomplish, only to find yourself 45 minutes later still slowly meandering around the beds and paths, simply taking it all in? For seemingly endless winter months, we excitedly anticipate the prospects of the upcoming season. Then, a mere month into it, we're already taking stock of what's working, what's not, what we miss having in the garden, what we're growing too much of . . . and jotting it all down with thoughts of next summer's garden. The tricky part is to find moments to set your mind free of all of that, and just to bask in the beauty that's before you—because that's where the magic is.

This is why it's important to have a good garden nook! As you plot and plan your garden, make sure to carve out a spot to sit and soak. A place to have your morning coffee or tea. A place to take in all the beauty you've sown and the flitting and buzzing visitors it attracts. A place where you sit for a few minutes during those moments when you need a respite.

It doesn't have to be anything fancy. Often, I find myself perching on a log, even though there's a perfectly good patio nearby. I do like to try to blend into the environment in hopes of witnessing the garden activity up close. I often tuck a chair beside a trellis for the best bird-watching. Birds love landing on the tops of the trellises, as it gives them a nice spot to rest with clear views all around; that allows them to scout their next food source while keeping an eye out for potential predators. If you don't have much garden space or are limited to growing in containers, you can still "nook it up." I spent several summers sitting happily next to my pots of herbs and flowers on my back stairs. The key is just to have a spot where you can go to sit still and take in a few minutes of simply being outside, in nature, with your gorgeous plants.

Planting equal amounts of herbs, vegetables, and flowers brought balance not only to the garden but to my life as well. It allowed more stolen moments for meandering in the garden.

Plant a Pollinator's Paradise

Garden pollinators come in all shapes and sizes. They're bees, wasps, moths, butterflies, birds, beetles, and even mosquitoes. All are vital for having a healthy, vibrant ecosystem. Here are a few tips for bringing in the pollinators.

❀ You can attract certain pollinators just by planting flowers of different colors. Bees love hues of blues, purples, yellows, and whites, while butterflies flock to reds, purples, and yellows.

❀ Flower shape is key to attracting pollinators. Double and ruffle blooms are beautiful, but pollinators prefer single-flowered varieties. Not only do the single flowers make it easier for beneficial creatures to collect the pollen and nectar, but those plants produce a higher amount of both when compared to double-blooming varieties. Tubular flowers such as honeysuckle, lupine, and anise hyssop attract pollinators with longer proboscises, like hummingbirds and moths.

❀ Plant your perennials in groupings of five to seven of the same variety. This allows the pollinators to easily collect pollen and nectar from a single species, which they prefer. Plus, grouping your flowers en masse creates striking visual displays.

❀ When plotting out your perennials, incorporate at least one-third native plants. Not only are natives adapted to grow in your climate, but they also attract more pollinators. If you're curious about the native plants in your area, visit your local university's Cooperative Extension Service website.

❀ Plan for a sequence of blooms so that pollinators have a source of nectar throughout the season. Early- and late-blooming perennials are especially important for our pollinator pals, as these are the times when their food sources are scarcest. In spring, pollinators awake from dormancy, and they need to refill their depleted energy reserves with nectar and pollen. Come fall, these same pollinators need to fill up with a few feasts before winter arrives.

❀ Provide a bee bath using a shallow dish, marbles, and fresh water for your bee friends to sip and to bring back to the hive.

SHOP LOCAL

There are so many reasons to grow native plants! The first and most obvious one is, they're native. That means they're equipped not only to grow but to *thrive* in your climate. Second, they serve as an important part of your home ecosystem, providing food and habitat not only to your pollinator friends but also to a whole host of other organisms. Third, native plants are low maintenance, if they're planted in a spot that offers their preferred growing conditions (dry, boggy, shady, sunny, etc.). Fourth, many native plants use less water than their foreign cousins do, helping conserve an incredibly valuable resource, but also making them more drought resistant. And last, they are total eye candy to have around your property.

BLOW FLIES
ON DAHLIA

APHRODITE FRITILLARY
ON ZINNIA

SWALLOWTAIL
BUTTERFLIES
ON CHIVES

Best Flowers
TO ATTRACT
POLLINATORS

Aster

Bee balm

Butterfly bush

Daisy

Echinacea

Globe gilia

Joe-Pye weed

Ornamental grasses

Phlox

Pincushion flower

Rudbeckia

Salvia

Sedum

Snapdragon

Verbena

Yarrow

Zinnia

Flowering herbs
(like chives, oregano,
thyme, and sage)

MONARCH ON
ECHINACEA

HUMMINGBIRD MOTH
ON BEE BALM

RUDBECKIA

Make a Bug Hotel

Create the perfect nook for all your beneficial insect pals to nest in over winter with this easy-to-make habitat. Your bug hotel will not only attract insects, but it may also become a home to frogs, toads, newts, even a small mammal or two.

Your bug hotel can be as small as a birdhouse or as large as you'd like. The key to making a good one is to use natural objects and reclaimed materials, like that pile of broken terra-cotta pots you've been collecting. Straw, moss, dry leaves, twigs, pinecones, and bark are other great items to include, especially because different materials attract different insects.

To make your own:

◆ Build a wooden frame that is 6 inches deep. You can make it shallower or deeper, but 6 to 8 inches has worked best for me.

◆ Add partitions in your frame to create cavities for different materials.

◆ Using chicken wire, enclose the back of the frame to keep the contents from falling out.

◆ Secure your frame to an elevated platform (we have ours on cinder blocks) or hang it from a wall, fence, or tree.

◆ Fill each cavity to capacity with your materials of choice. Don't pack the materials in tight, but do create a snug enough space that the contents won't shift around much. To help hold in wobbly items like pinecones, secure them to the front of the cavity with some chicken wire.

◆ Place the finished bug hotel in a sunny, sheltered spot that's close to your garden.

◆ Hang smaller bug hotels from trees or on trellises.

Mason Bee Nesting House

Support your native bee population and send your pollination rates skyrocketing by including a mason bee house near your garden. Unlike honeybees, mason bees do not make honey, but they do make a powerful impact on your garden success with their pollination prowess. These solitary dwellers are native bees that seek out hollow stems of plants to lay their eggs in.

To make your own:

◆ Collect materials with hollow stems, like bamboo, raspberry or blackberry canes, sunflower stalks, or reeds.

◆ Cut the materials into 8-inch lengths and bundle together in groups of 15 to 20 pieces.

◆ Tie the bundles together tightly using jute or wire.

Another option is:

◆ Drill several $\frac{5}{16}$-inch holes 6 inches deep into an untreated block of wood. The diameter of the hole is important—$\frac{5}{16}$ inch is the space a mason bee seeks out to lay its eggs.

◆ Mount your mason bee house in a secure spot not too far from your garden—on the side of your home, a tree, or anywhere else that feels the warmth of the southern sun and offers protection from strong wind and rain.

Companion Planting

Companion planting is what made me leave the land of straight and tidy rows and led me to my vibrant jumble of garden happiness. It has made all the difference in my garden; not only do these planting partnerships benefit each crop, but they also attract pollinators, mitigate disease and pest populations, and create the most charming display of plants. In a nutshell, plant veggies, flowers, and herbs all together in one bed for symbiotic happiness, as well as for some incredibly stunning garden landscaping.

If you're ever in doubt about which plants to grow together, follow the garden adage of "Things that go together well in the kitchen grow together well in the same garden bed." In other words, that same combination of tomato, basil, onion, and oregano that makes a delightful sauce also gets along wonderfully when interplanted.

Here are a few of my favorite companion combinations.

Cabbage + Kale + Chamomile + Sage + Dill

- Dill improves cabbage growth and attracts predatory wasps that target cabbageworms.

- Chamomile gives brassicas a flavor boost.
- Chamomile boosts cabbage and kale's health and growth.

- Sage wards off the small white butterfly that lays cabbageworm eggs.

Tomato + Basil + Borage + Alliums + Calendula

- Basil repels tomato pests like hornworms and aphids while attracting bees to come hither and pollinate the tomatoes.

- The strong scent of alliums helps deter insect pests from tomatoes.

- Calendula and borage keep tomato hornworms at bay and attract pollinators.

Bush Beans + Summer Savory + Rosemary + Carrots + Cucumbers

- ◆ Summer savory boosts carrot's flavor and growth and helps repel pests.

- ◆ Carrots add a boost to the growth of bush beans.
- ◆ Bush beans and cucumbers benefit each other mutually.

- ◆ Rosemary wards off carrot-rust fly.

Cabbage + Violas + Rosemary + Thyme + Geraniums

A border of violas, along with the other aromatic herbs, confuses pests with strong scents, protecting your cabbage.

Broccoli + Calendula + Celery + Chamomile + Alyssum

Celery, herbs, and alyssum repel cabbageworms and give brassicas a growth boost while chamomile is said to enhance broccoli's flavor.

Carrots + Onions + Radishes + Rosemary + Leeks

The pungent aroma of rosemary, onions, and leeks repels carrot-rust fly, while quick-growing radishes help loosen the soil for those root veggies to form.

Peas + Carrots + Cucumbers + Radishes + Nasturtiums

- Peas feed the soil with nitrogen.
- Radishes and nasturtiums repel cucumber beetles.
- Radishes help break up the soil and encourage the carrot's germination and root formation.

Three Sisters: Corn + Pole Beans + Squash

- Corn supports the vining pole beans.
- Pole beans feed the soil.
- Squash controls the weeds and keeps the soil moist.

A Few Other Favorites:

- Any fruiting vegetable planted with annual flowers will be better pollinated and have better fruit set.
- Nasturtiums and thyme repel cucumber beetles and attract predatory insects.
- Chives deter many pests and are said to improve carrot's taste and growth.
- Mint and oregano attract ladybugs and lacewings.
- Chamomile attracts parasitic wasps.
- Dill attracts predator wasps.
- Rosemary repels cabbage moths.

FOES, NOT FRIENDS
Plants to Keep Away from Each Other

Beans and peas aren't good with brassicas. The excess nitrogen that beans release can cause broccoli to develop a hollow stem.

Dill negatively affects carrot's growth.

Keep heavy feeders like strawberries, tomatoes, and pole beans away from your broccoli, cabbage, Brussels sprouts, cauliflower, and kale because they will compete for nutrients.

Alliums like onions and garlic can stunt the growth of peas and beans.

Brassicas are said to inhibit the growth of tomatoes.

Battling Garden Pests & Disease

Nothing breaks a gardener's heart more than losing a beloved plant, raised so carefully from seed, to pest or disease. Truth be told, I think it's been a good 12 years since I lost *all* my tomatoes to late blight, and I'm still not 100 percent over it. The hard reality of battling these garden foes is that much of it is out of your control, and the best you can do is try to mitigate the damage.

Following are a few familiar pests, along with my go-tos for arming myself against them.

Squirrels

Turns out, squirrels aren't spice fans. After years of endless squirrel invasions on my bird feeders and all around my garden, help finally arrived in the form of red pepper flakes. Shake the flakes in your birdseed and around your seedlings to ward off those furry little menaces. The birds will pay no mind, but the squirrels will definitely not be fans of the spice.

Deer

The best deer deterrent I've ever used has also been the simplest—fishing line. Around your garden perimeter, string a border of fishing line 1 foot above the ground. The deer can't see it but can feel it and will not cross the border. It does keep the deer out, but be mindful: This is a huge tripping hazard for yourself and any other human garden visitors as well!

Slugs

Water plants in the morning, so that come evening, the soil surface will be dry during the slugs' active time; they're not fans of dry soil. You can also sprinkle crushed eggshells or diatomaceous earth around the plants as a good deterrent.

Cabbage-Root Maggots

Of all the garden pests I've battled, this foe is the cruelest. Cabbage-root flies lay eggs around the base of the plant (cole crops in particular) in early spring and again in late summer; they prefer cool northern gardens with rich soil. The larvae tunnel to the root system, destroying the plant. The scary part is that all of this goes on undetected aboveground until it is pretty much too late. One day you notice something just isn't right with your plants. They suddenly appear wilted and withered. Heartbreakingly, by then there is no saving them.

I've found that delaying planting until early June avoids exposing plants to the mid-May egg-laying fiesta. Placing row covers over the plants helps, but only if you're sure there are no cabbage-root maggots in the soil already; if there are, the row covers will trap them in. A cardboard collar placed firmly around the base of each plant blocks adults from laying their eggs by the stem. Bringing in nematodes is another option, but you will need to buy a lot of them. And though I generally don't till, this is one instance when using a scuffle hoe to give the beds a gentle turn may be in order. Root maggots overwinter in the first few inches of soil, eagerly awaiting spring when the adults emerge and invade. By tilling 7 inches deep in both fall and spring, you disturb their environment, hopefully squashing their population for the next season.

Cabbageworms

Keep an eye out early in the season for small white butterflies: They're seeking your brassicas to lay their eggs on. Their eggs become those nasty cabbageworms. You can use a butterfly net to nab them before they become too comfortable in your garden. Floating row covers are the easiest protection, but make sure to cover your plants *before* you spy that first white butterfly, otherwise the butterfly will have an opportunity to lay its eggs on the plant. Companion planting with calendula is also helpful. The most effective action is diligently checking the back of each brassica leaf for cabbageworm eggs and destroying them. It's very time consuming, but it works.

Cucumber Beetles and Bacterial Wilt

Ever gone to bed saying goodnight to your beautiful cucumber or squash plants, only to wake up the next morning to sad, wilting shadows of those plants? Chances are they got infected by bacterial wilt. Cucumber beetles transmit bacterial wilt by biting the plants' leaves.

To help prevent this heartbreak, arm yourself with cotton swabs, petroleum jelly, and a cup of soapy water. Either in the early morning or late evening, head out to the garden and begin your hunt, as the beetles are groggy at these times of day and much easier to catch. Simply swirl a cotton swab in a bit of petroleum jelly and nab the bad guys by tapping them with the swab; the beetles will stick to the jelly. Drop the beetle into the cup of soapy water.

Another option is to mix kaolin clay and water in a spray bottle and mist infested plants. This will leave a powdery, gray film on your plants that the beetles find unattractive for both eating and laying eggs. This spray should be reapplied after heavy rains, and you'll need to be sure to spray the undersides of leaves as well.

Bee Mindful of Other Pollinators While Battling Garden Pests

In our quest to battle the bad pests in our gardens, we may unintentionally harm beneficial insects. Before you spray any plant, even when using all-natural organic sprays, be mindful of the surrounding environment. Check those squash blossoms for sleepy bees before you spray; look under leaves for frogs and friends; and watch for caterpillars, as many of these will become prolific pollinators that you'll want to keep around. If you're spraying at night, remember that bats are pollinators, too, and evenings are when they're active.

What Tomato Hornworms Grow Up to Be

Did you know that those big, creepy tomato hornworms grow up to be huge, quite beautiful moths? The caterpillars are the larvae of the five-spotted hawk moth, a gray-and-brown insect. Once you see what these creatures transform into, you may want to simply pick the hornworms off your tomatoes and rehome them near nicotiana or phlox plants (other favored foods) rather than squashing them.

Each fall, the caterpillars burrow down into the soil to pupate. After overwintering in the soil, they wiggle their way back to the surface, emerging as moths in spring. The mature caterpillars drop off plants and burrow into the soil to pupate. Moths emerge in 2 weeks to begin a second generation during midsummer. It's the second generation of moths that deposit eggs on host plants like your tomatoes, which they'll feed on until it's time to pupate and the whole cycle begins again.

Write down the parts of the garden that bring you the most joy, and make sure to grow lots more of that next year.

Keeping a Garden Journal

Gardening is personal. What seems to grow well for everyone else may not thrive for you. You may even struggle to grow something that your neighbor grows effortlessly. By keeping track of your garden successes and challenges each season (along with a weather log), you'll be able to spot patterns over time. Some will be obvious, like the annual entries about your struggles with a certain plant; for me, it's always been cauliflower. If it hasn't grown successfully year after year, it's probably not going to. Other entries may point to weather being a cause for success or failure, like noticing that the rainy years were when you rocked your root veggie harvests, but they were also when your tomatoes suffered, and vice versa. All this information will be beyond helpful when it comes time to plan next year's garden.

Here are a few things to consider keeping in your journal.

🌼 A simple garden map marked with which crops were grown where (crucial for plotting crop rotations).

🌼 Monthly observations of what's growing well and what isn't, along with notes of possible causes (such as weather or pests).

🌼 A log of which varieties grew best, along with the results of any taste tests.

🌼 Notes about when flowers are in bloom.

🌼 Lists of plant groupings that you really enjoyed, or companion planting partners that seemed to sing.

🌼 Wildlife and insect observations. Your garden is its own ecosystem. Keep a guest book of your favorite visitors and note their arrivals and departures.

🌼 Observations about pest arrivals and departures. After years of observing, I can practically predict when the cabbage moths will arrive and thus thwart them before they lay eggs on my beloved brassicas.

BEANS

Every year I tell myself to plant fewer beans, and every year I end up planting more than ever. The only really hard part about growing beans is narrowing down which cultivars to choose.

WHEN TO SOW Direct sow once the soil has warmed, usually 3 weeks after the last frost date.

SOIL Compost-rich soil

PREFERRED LIGHT Full sun

Tips + Tricks

GROWING

- Companion plant with beets, calendula, carrots, celery, corn, cucumbers, potatoes, and summer savory. Beans are not fans of basil, fennel, garlic, and onions.

- Wait until your soil warms to at least 70°F/21°C before sowing in a sunny spot because beans are warm-season lovers. If you receive more than 8 hours of full sun, part shade may suit them better.

- Boost your soil's nitrogen content simply by growing beans. No fertilizer is ever needed, as beans produce their own nitrogen that in turn feeds the soil. When a bean plant dies back, cut it off at ground level to remove the stem and leaves, but keep the roots in the soil. They will slowly release that precious nitrogen to make the next round of crops in that bed very happy.

HARVESTING

- Harvest snap bean pods when they are young and tender. Harvest shell beans when the pods are bulging and you can see the outline of the seeds in the pod.

- Pick your pods often. The more pods you pick, the more pods the plants will produce.

- Sow seeds every 2 weeks for a continual harvest all season long.

- Avoid touching the plants when they are wet; diseases are easily spread when plants are damp.

'DRAGON'S TONGUE'

'ROYAL BURGUNDY'

Favorite Varieties

BUSH: 'Gold Rush', 'Royal Burgundy', 'Red Swan', 'Dragon's Tongue', 'Borlotto di Vigevano Nano'

POLE: 'Trionfo Violetto', 'Kentucky Wonder'

HARICOT VERTS: French type with pencil-thin, rounded, delicious pods like 'Masai' or 'Maxibel'

SOYBEANS: 'Butterbean', 'Beer Friend', 'Envy'

RUBY-THROATED HUMMINGBIRD ON SCARLET RUNNER BEANS

'BORLOTTO DI VIGEVANO NANO'

DILLY BEANS

When my family first moved to Maine, our neighbors, the Archers, welcomed us with homemade raspberry jam and a jar of dilly beans. Having never heard of dilly beans before, we were introduced to a whole new world of garden-fresh goodness and preserving. The Archers were amazing folks whose talents at all things homesteading never ceased to amaze or inspire me. I think of them often as I'm out in the garden—especially come bean season.

MAKES 1 QUART

- 2   cups green beans, blanched
- ½   small onion, thinly sliced
- ½   teaspoon black peppercorns
- ¼   teaspoon red pepper flakes

FOR THE BRINE
- ¾   cup distilled white vinegar
- ¾   cup water
- 2   tablespoons sugar
- 1   garlic clove, minced
- 1   teaspoon kosher salt
- 2   dill sprigs

Make the brine: Combine the vinegar, water, sugar, garlic, and salt in a medium covered saucepan. Bring to a boil over medium-high heat, then remove the pan from the heat. Wrap the dill sprigs in cheesecloth and add them to the brine mixture. Let the dill steep for 15 minutes, then discard it. (If left to steep longer, the dill becomes bitter.) Let the brine cool to room temperature.

Pack the beans, onion, peppercorns, and pepper flakes into a sterilized widemouthed quart jar, then pour the cooled brine over them. Attach a nonreactive lid and refrigerate the beans for 2 weeks before eating. Give the jar a gentle shake every few days during that time. Store in the refrigerator for up to 3 months.

SOYBEANS

Also known as edamame, these interactive pods of *yum* have been a hit in my family since my boys were toddlers. It was an easy way for them to learn to like their veggies; soybeans are not only tasty but can also be shot across the table at one's brother simply by pressing the outer shell and playfully popping out the seed inside.

GROWING

◆ Give soybean plants room to grow, as they get much bigger and branch more than bush beans.

HARVESTING

◆ Pick right before dinnertime for the best taste. Because their flavor peaks in the evening, soybeans are the exception to the garden rule of harvesting vegetables in the morning.

◆ Watch those pods! Soybeans have a relatively short window of picking opportunity, and they go from being ready to being past their peak in just a few days.

◆ Pick pods as soon as they're bright green and plump. If they're yellow, they're past their window a bit, but still good to eat; they just won't be as nutrient-packed, and their texture will be starchier.

◆ Freeze the bounty by blanching the pods in boiling salted water for 1 minute, then plunging them into ice water to stop the cooking process. Drain, dry, and freeze in ziplock bags.

EATING

◆ Make a quick-and-easy snack or side dish by microwaving the pods in a covered bowl for 4 minutes. Top with a sprinkling of salt and enjoy.

◆ Let some pods dry fully on the plant and harvest the seeds inside for use as excellent dried beans, too.

What's the Difference between Pole and Bush Beans?

Bush beans tend to come into picking fast and furious and then quickly shut down 3 to 4 weeks later, which makes them great for succession sowing. Pole beans, on the other hand, are generally harvested in a 6- to 8-week period.

SUMMER SQUASH & ZUCCHINI

There are so many great varieties of squash to grow, it's often hard to stick to my golden rule of "No more than two squash plants." But that rule is there for a reason, rightfully earned when a single pattypan squash plant—just one!—produced over 40 fruit one summer.

WHEN TO SOW Direct sow once the soil has warmed, or start indoors 2–4 weeks before the last frost date.

SOIL Compost-rich soil kept evenly moist, but not soaked

PREFERRED LIGHT Full sun

'ZEPHYR'

'COCOZELLE'

Favorite Varieties

ZUCCHINI: 'Cocozelle', 'Costata Romanesco', 'Raven'

YELLOW: 'Cube of Butter'

PATTYPAN: 'Sunburst', 'Benning's Green Tint'

PATTYPAN

✗✗ EAT

SAVOR THOSE SEEDS

Roasting squash seeds isn't just for Halloween. Whether it's a summer or winter squash or a pumpkin, save all its seeds and roast them into nutty deliciousness for snacking or sprinkling onto whatever is for dinner. Toss the seeds with a drizzle of olive oil or melted butter and a pinch of salt, then spread in a single layer on a baking sheet. Bake in a preheated 300°F/150°C oven for 35 to 45 minutes, or until golden brown.

GROWING

◆ Companion plant with the Three Sisters. A traditional planting technique of Indigenous peoples of North America, the Three Sisters groups corn, pole beans, and squash together in the same growing area. Each plant benefits the other: Pole beans grow up the corn and help reinvigorate the soil after squash and corn's heavy feeding; squash controls the weeds.

◆ Add a good dollop of compost to the bed prior to transplanting squash.

◆ Plan to succession sow another crop once your summer squash harvest is done. Fast-growing squash plants are harvested well before the first frost date, making their growing space the perfect spot for a later-season succession planting of short-season crops like lettuce, radish, or bush beans.

◆ Prevent powdery mildew by watering at the base of the plant, and avoid wetting the leaves.

◆ Help prevent blossom-end rot. When the fruits begin to swell in girth and grow, pinch off the blossom that is still connected to the fruit. While pretty, that blossom can easily develop a fungus that, if left on, can infect the fruit.

◆ Feed with a small helping of nitrogen if the leaves are yellowing. Avoid overfertilizing, as that will produce more leaves and less fruit.

◆ Provide good airflow during the dog days of summer by cutting off old, yellowing leaves. You can even place a tomato cage over the plants when they are seedlings to help keep the squash leaves off the ground.

HARVESTING

◆ Harvest when squash fruits are young. Keep a watchful eye, as legend goes that a summer squash can grow a foot overnight.

◆ Pick often to spur more production.

PEST CONTROL

◆ Deter cucumber beetles and squash bugs by sowing a few radish seeds around each squash plant. Leave those radishes for the lifespan of your squash. Let them flower and go to seed, then nibble on their delectable, crispy radish seedpods.

◆ Ward off squash vine borers by covering the base of the plant, the borers' favorite target. You can use row cover or mulch to protect the base.

EAT

SUMMER SQUASH, JALAPEÑO & FETA FRITTERS

These quick-and-easy fritters are so tasty, they'll quickly put to good use that hoard of summer squash filling up your refrigerator. And they're so versatile, you can have them for any meal—topped with an egg for breakfast, served on a hearty wheat roll for lunch, or as the perfect partner with pretty much anything for dinner.

SERVES 4

- 2 large summer squash or zucchini (or a combination of both)
- 1 teaspoon kosher salt (or Rosemary-Lemon Salt from page 163)
- ½ cup all-purpose flour
- ½ teaspoon baking powder
- ¼ teaspoon freshly ground black pepper

- 2 tablespoons fresh parsley, finely chopped
- 2 scallions, finely chopped
- 2 garlic cloves, minced
- 1 jalapeño, finely chopped
- 1 large egg, lightly beaten
- 2 ounces feta cheese, crumbled
- ⅓ cup extra virgin olive oil
- 1 lemon, halved

1 Grate the squash into a fine-mesh strainer and sprinkle with ½ teaspoon of the salt. Place the strainer over a large bowl and let the squash drain for 20 minutes.

2 Mix the flour, baking powder, black pepper, and remaining ½ teaspoon salt in a small bowl. Set aside.

3 Squeeze the excess liquid from the squash. Dispose of the liquid and transfer the squash to a large bowl. Add the parsley, scallions, garlic, and jalapeño. Gently fold in the egg, then the cheese. Add the flour mixture and fold together until fully moistened.

4 Heat the oil in a skillet over medium-high heat until hot but not smoking. Gently drop large spoonfuls of the fritter batter into the skillet, pressing down on each fritter with a spatula to flatten it for even cooking. Cook for 4 to 5 minutes, then flip and cook until golden brown, about 5 minutes longer. If frying in batches, keep the cooked fritters warm in a 225°F/110°C oven. To serve, squeeze the lemon halves over the fritters and enjoy.

EAT THE MALES

Learn the difference between a male and a female flower for two good reasons: to boost pollination and for snacking!

Take a gander at your flowers. Do you see how some form close to the base of the plant, while others form off longer stalks? The ones on the longer stalks are the males. If you want to ensure pollination, gently tickle the stamen of the male flower with a small paint-brush (you'll see golden pollen collect on the brush). Carefully open the female flower to expose the stigma and brush the pollen onto it with a few soft strokes.

Treat yourself to a culinary delight by harvesting a few of the male flowers. Stuff them with ricotta cheese and herbs, dredge lightly in flour, then panfry for a few minutes until golden brown.

CARROTS

I'll admit it—I never really grow huge, long carrots. Rather, I'm more of a master of growing small to medium-size carrots. I used to think that some growing error or lack of soil love caused this. Turns out, the culprit is my complete and continued lack of patience to let these sweet garden snacks of happiness grow longer. I start plucking them as soon as I spy the first hint of a carrot shoulder pushing up through the soil surface and immediately devour them. (This is also the reason why my carrots rarely make it into the kitchen.)

WHEN TO SOW
Direct sow 2 to 3 weeks before the last frost date.

SOIL Compost-rich, well-drained soil; mixing in a helping of sand would be a welcomed addition to create looser soil

PREFERRED LIGHT
Full sun

Favorite Varieties

MY GO-TO CARROTS: Over the years, I've planted dozens of different carrot varieties, but 'Scarlet Nantes', 'Nelson', 'Mokum', 'Napoli', 'Purple Haze', and 'Rainbow' will always have a place in my garden.

FOR A LITTLE COLOR FUN: I love sowing a few patches of 'Carnival Blend' and 'Atomic Red'.

FOR CONTAINER GROWING: Try 'Parisian', 'Little Finger', or other baby varieties.

Tips + Tricks

◆ Always companion plant with radishes. The radishes help keep the soil loose, which is great for the carrots' root formation. Carrots also interplant well with onions and leeks; both help repel the dreaded carrot-rust fly.

◆ Keep your carrots happy by ensuring they get 1 inch of water per week. Carrots don't like it when the soil gets too dry, which can affect root development.

◆ Avoid sowing in the peak of summer's heat. Cool-weather-loving carrots will not form quality roots when soil temperatures rise above 75°F/24°C.

◆ Pinch or use scissors when thinning young seedlings; uprooting them can disturb the neighboring seedlings' delicate roots.

◆ Sow a row of carrots every 2 to 3 weeks to keep yourself in carrot happiness for months on end.

◆ Grow a full season of carrots in one sowing by looking for varieties that are ready for harvest at different points in the season. Carrots come in short-season, midseason, and long-season varieties. The long-season ones are best for storage.

◆ Keep your freshly picked carrots crisp in storage by cutting off the foliage, leaving just an inch of the stem. While carrots and radishes look beautiful with their leaves on, the reality is that those greens suck up the root's moisture, resulting in spongy vegetables.

◆ Prevent damage from carrot-rust flies by always sowing seed in a new bed location each year, using row covers, companion planting with alliums like leeks and onions, and sowing midseason after the first egg-laying period is over.

'MOKUM'

'ATOMIC RED'

LITTLE FINGER

NANTES

CUCUMBERS

There's something about the refreshing crispness of a good garden cucumber that takes the sizzle out of the hottest summer days. I nosh on these delights in all sorts of ways, but my daily go-to during the season is tossing a few slices into my water, along with some sprigs of mint, for a quenching drink to sip all day.

WHEN TO SOW
Direct sow once the soil has warmed, or start indoors 2–4 weeks before the last frost date.

SOIL
Compost-rich, well-drained soil

PREFERRED LIGHT
Full sun

Favorite Varieties

PICKLERS:
'Northern Pickling', 'Little Leaf', 'Persian Baby'

SALAD SLICERS:
'Marketmore' and 'Diva' are divine.

UNIQUE FINDS:
Lemon cucumbers, cucamelons, and spiny cucumbers

SMALL-SPACE SOLUTIONS:
Grow bush varieties like 'Spacemaster', 'Bush Champion', or 'Salad Bush' or pickling varieties. Picklers grow great in containers.

Tips + Tricks

GROWING

- Companion plant with peas, beans, radishes, carrots, onions, corn, oregano, calendula, and nasturtium.

- Start your seeds off right by giving them the heat they need to germinate. Place your seed-starting trays in a warm location, like on top of your refrigerator, or use a seedling heat mat.

- Avoid transplant shock by starting your indoor-sown seeds in containers that can be directly transplanted into the garden; cucumbers don't like root disturbance.

- Succession sow every 3 weeks for a continual harvest all season long.

- Feed with a good helping of liquid tomato fertilizer when the plants begin to flower.

- Provide 1 inch of water per week. To discourage fungal diseases, avoid wetting the foliage; instead, water around the base of the plant.

- Pinch out the cucumber plant's growing tip when it climbs to the top of its trellis to encourage the development of side shoots.

HARVESTING

- Harvest in the cool of the morning and be sure to pick often; the more you harvest, the more fruits the plants will produce.

'LITTLE LEAF'

'MARKETMORE'

'ITACHI'

EAT

REFRIGERATOR PICKLES

I realized early on that I was not a canning kind of gal, no matter how much I aspired to be. So refrigerator pickles are a perfect fit for me. These crispy delights can last up to 6 months in the refrigerator, and you don't have all the fuss and muss of canning. You'll also find that infusing the dill and vinegar together before pouring them over the vegetables really changes your pickling game by maximizing all of dill's delicious flavor.

Experiment beyond cucumbers. This brine works great with all sorts of vegetables. Depending on what is ready for harvest, I often use a mix of garden veggies, including peppers, carrots, peas, and radishes.

MAKES 1 GALLON

2	cups distilled white vinegar
¾	cup sugar
¼	cup kosher salt
2	teaspoons dill seed
1	teaspoon mustard seed
	Several dill sprigs
10	pickling cucumbers, sliced as desired
1	medium onion, thinly sliced
2	medium jalapeños, sliced (for a little spice with your pickles; optional)
4	garlic cloves, thinly sliced

1 Combine the vinegar, sugar, salt, dill seed, and mustard seed in a small saucepan and bring to a simmer, then remove the pan from the heat.

2 Wrap the dill sprigs in a piece of cheesecloth and add it to the vinegar mixture. Let steep for 10 to 12 minutes, then discard the dill. (If left to steep longer, the dill becomes bitter.)

3 Layer the cucumbers, onion, jalapeños, and garlic into two sterilized ½-gallon canning jars. Divide the vinegar mixture equally between the jars. The mixture will not cover the cucumbers at first, but the cucumbers will release water as they sit in the refrigerator.

4 Using plastic or other nonreactive lids, cover the jars tightly. Keep in the refrigerator for up to 6 months, giving the jars an occasional gentle shake or two.

BASIL

Your tomatoes would be lonely without basil, so you really must grow this wonderful companion plant. Don't plant it out in the garden until the soil and temperatures have warmed, otherwise you risk being crushed when cold temps turn basil into a mess of blackened leaves.

WHEN TO SOW Start indoors 6 to 8 weeks before the last frost date and transplant once the soil has warmed up, or direct sow once the soil warms.

SOIL
Rich, well-drained, moist soil

PREFERRED LIGHT
Full sun to part shade

Tips + Tricks

- Companion plant with tomatoes and lettuce, as basil improves the flavor of both.

- Protect these tender annuals from cold temperatures by covering with a row cover when temperatures dip below 40°F/5°C. Even the lightest frost can blacken basil's leaves.

- Succession sow every 2 to 3 weeks for continuous harvests throughout the season.

- Space plants 12 inches apart to allow for good air circulation, which helps control the spread of mildew.

- Provide 1 inch of water a week to keep the soil moist, allowing the plant's roots to flourish and ensuring that your basil won't wilt.

- Pinch back basil often to encourage bushier plants, which produce more tasty leaves.

- Mulch to help keep the soil moist and cool.

- Prevent the spread of disease by watering basil plants from below, and avoid wetting the leaves.

- Put away the fertilizer, as it makes the leaves less flavorful.

Medicinal Properties

Antibacterial, anti-inflammatory, high in antioxidants

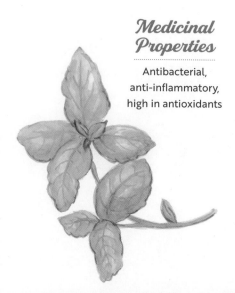

'GENOVESE' AND 'DARK OPAL'

TULSI

Favorite Varieties

TULSI. Also known as holy basil, this basil has an incredible scent and is revered in Ayurvedic medicine. It brews up a delicious and beneficial tea.

'LETTUCE LEAF'. Big, lush leaves are perfect for layering with mozzarella and your favorite heirloom tomato, or use them as a wrap and get rolling.

'SPICY GLOBE'. Tiny leaves mound up in a petite, perfect globe: great for pots or the front of a border.

'PURPLE PETRA'. This packs a purple punch sure to brighten any planting combination. It's a bit milder than its green counterparts.

'MRS. BURNS' LEMON'. The only way you could improve on basil's perfection is with this variety's tangy, citrus punch.

'PURPLE PETRA'

CINNAMON BASIL

Making the Most of Your Basil Bounty

When it comes time to harvest your beautiful basil, be sure to process it carefully to preserve its flavor.

◆ Don't bother drying basil—it loses much of its flavor when dried.

◆ Layer whole basil leaves into an airtight container, lightly sprinkling with salt between layers, then cover with olive oil. Store the container in the freezer. The basil-infused oil is a delicious side product.

◆ Blanch for a few seconds in boiling water (to preserve the color). Squeeze dry and freeze.

◆ Flash freeze whole leaves on the stem, then seal in an airtight container and store in the freezer.

◆ Avoid cutting basil with metal, as metal causes the leaves to oxidize, giving the basil an off taste. Rather, tear basil with your hands.

◆ When cooking, add basil at the very end of the recipe for the best flavor.

◆ Extend your bounty by storing stems of fresh basil in a jar of water on the counter, just like you would cut flowers. Change the water daily.

BASIL INSECT REPELLANT

Maine and mosquitoes are synonymous. I'd love to say that's an exaggeration, but it's really not. Thankfully, there's something in the garden that can help keep bugs at bay. Basil's volatile compounds, like citronella and limonene, disrupt mosquitoes' senses, making the bugs too confused to nibble on you. To harness those volatile oils, however, you need to extract them from the plant. You can either crush some basil leaves and rub them directly on your skin, or you can make this infusion to have on hand whenever you need it.

    6   ounces fresh basil leaves and stems
    4   ounces boiling water
    4   ounces vodka*

Place the basil in a glass container and pour the boiling water over it. Cover and let sit for 6 hours. Strain out and discard the basil and pour the infused water into an 8-ounce spray bottle. Pour the vodka into the bottle and gently shake. Store in a cool, dark spot. Avoid spraying around the face, and keep out of reach of little ones.

*The vodka helps preserve the repellant. If you choose to omit it, make small batches of basil-infused water and keep them in the refrigerator for 5 to 7 days.

HERB PASTA DOUGH

Incorporating fresh herbs into pasta dough not only adds a bite of garden deliciousness to your dish, it can also create an enchanting visual impact at your dinner table. You'll need room to spread out to make this recipe; a large countertop or table is ideal.

MAKES 1 POUND OF PASTA

- 2¼ cups all-purpose flour, plus more for dusting
- 3 eggs
- ¾ teaspoon salt
- 1 tablespoon olive oil, plus more for the bowl
- 1 tablespoon lukewarm water
  Handful of tender fresh herbs (such as basil, chives, sage, oregano, and parsley)

1 Lightly dust the work surface with a small handful of flour. In the center of the workspace, mound the flour. Make a well in the center of the mound and add the eggs, salt, oil, and water. Begin to mix the wet ingredients, gradually incorporating a bit of flour as you mix, until a rough dough starts to form. Knead for a few more turns, then place the dough in an oiled bowl and cover with plastic wrap. Let the dough rest for 20 to 30 minutes.

2 Using a pasta machine or rolling pin, roll out the dough into long flat sheets ¹⁄₁₆ inch thick. Slice the sheets into workable lengths. Lay one sheet on the lightly floured work surface and arrange herbs on it, as desired.

3 Place a second sheet of dough on top. Gently but firmly, press down to adhere the top sheet to the bottom. If the two sheets of dough aren't sticking together well, gently pull back the top layer, lightly mist with water, and try again.

4 Feed the combined sheet of dough through the pasta machine a few times, or roll with a rolling pin. Place the herbed dough sheet on the lightly floured surface, and cut into desired shapes. Use immediately or store tightly wrapped in the refrigerator for up to two days. Cooking time varies depending on the shape of the pasta, but is generally 3–5 minutes.

HERB PASTE

Toss a handful of basil leaves into a food processor and pulse until the herbs are finely chopped. Drizzle with olive oil and process until the mixture becomes a smooth paste. Pour into ice cube trays and freeze. Remove the frozen cubes from the tray and store in the freezer in an airtight container. Use whenever you need a tasty shot of basil.

LAVENDER

It took me years to achieve success growing lavender in the garden. The first key was finding the right variety to grow for my hardiness zone. And the second was to stop growing it in compost-rich beds. This herb craves sandy, rocky, slightly acidic soil.

WHEN TO SOW Difficult to grow from seed and often not true to type. Best propagated via stem cuttings, or purchase seedlings.

SOIL Sandy, rocky, slightly acidic soil

PREFERRED LIGHT Full sun

Tips + Tricks

GROWING

- Set yourself up for lavender success by growing the right perennial for your zone—English in Zones 5 to 7, Spanish and French in Zones 8 and 9.

- Companion plant with brassicas to deter cabbageworms and next to fruit trees to boost their pollination.

- Sprinkle pebbles around the base of the herb to help provide good drainage, which is important to lavender's happiness.

- Try eating the flowers. Lavender's volatile oils, which deliver so many medicinal benefits, are also responsible for its bitter flavor. When used sparingly, though, lavender can add a lovely aroma to baked goods, syrups, and teas.

- Prune in early summer when you see new growth emerging, cutting out old, broken stems. Do not prune back in late summer: Lavender needs to save its energy for overwintering, and you don't want to encourage it to send out late-season new growth that can be damaged by cold winter temperatures.

HARVESTING

- Plan on harvesting only a few blooms for the first year or two from transplanting. This is something I learned from a gardening mentor a number of years ago. While practicing patience will be hard, you'll be rewarded with larger, bushier, more prolific plants. Lavender doesn't reach its full size or highest yields until the plant is three years old.

- Harvest the flowers right before they open; they'll keep their scent for months.

- Hang flower stems in loose bunches to dry, out of direct light in a well-ventilated area.

Medicinal Properties

Antibacterial, antiseptic, antimicrobial, antifungal, antispasmodic, anti-inflammatory

Favorite Varieties

There are around 30 different species of lavender. Sticking with English lavender (*Lavandula angustifolia*)—in particular, varieties such as 'Hidcote' and 'Munstead'—has been one key to my success with growing lavender in Zone 5. These varieties are the hardiest and can withstand temperatures of –20°F/–29°C. Folks in warmer climates can try the French and Spanish types.

If you're growing lavender for medicinal benefits, it's best to grow English lavender. There are lots of lovely hybrids out there—such as 'Lavandin', which has a wonderful aroma—but they don't offer the same medicinal punch. They are perfect for making home scents and cleaners, though.

FRENCH LAVENDER

NOURISH

LAVENDER-THYME TUB TEA

I had a short-lived dream of visiting one of those fabulous wellness spas. When I looked up the cost of a stay, the very long string of numbers after the dollar sign made me realize I could grow huge amounts of medicinal herbs for a tiny fraction of the spa expense. That spurred me to research what goes into all those magical products spas are known for. Turns out, I'm growing all the herbs I need, and I have the rest of the ingredients right in the kitchen. In other words, you can make your own wellness spa magic at home for about the price of a really good cup of coffee.

This one is a real soother. Tub teas create a bath infused with skin-soothing oatmeal, muscle-relaxing Epsom salts, and aromatic herbs that allow you to enjoy your own spa experience at home.

MAKES FIVE 2-OUNCE BAGS

4	ounces oatmeal, coarsely ground
4	ounces Epsom salts
2½	ounces dried lavender, crushed
2½	ounces dried thyme, crushed
1	ounce honey powder (to soften skin; optional)
¼	ounce dried orange peel, ground
1	ounce baking soda
8	drops lavender essential oil (optional)
6	drops thyme essential oil (optional)

Mix together the oatmeal, Epsom salts, lavender, thyme, honey powder, and orange peel in a large bowl.

Put the baking soda in a small bowl. Add the essential oils, if using, and thoroughly incorporate (this will evenly distribute the essential oils throughout the tub tea mixture). Add the baking soda mixture to the oatmeal mixture and stir to combine.

Divide the mixture into five small muslin sacks that can be tied closed. Alternatively, store the mixture in a glass jar.

TO USE: When drawing a warm bath, hang a muslin sack under the faucet as the tub fills, or spoon 3 to 4 tablespoons of the mixture into a tea strainer and hold under the faucet. If using a muslin sack, you can gently rub the sachet over your skin to exfoliate it.

Help control aphids, hornworms, and squash bugs by growing this beneficial insect-attracting herb nearby.

DILL

Do I make dozens of jars of refrigerator pickles because I like pickles or because I really, really like dill? All garden herbs are taste explosions, but something about freshly picked dill stands out. Perhaps it's such a delicate herb that the preserved version doesn't deliver that bright, unbridled bite that the plant offers straight from the garden. It's also quite a beckoning herb to your eye and to pollinators; it adds instant loveliness to any back-border planting.

Favorite Varieties

'FERNLEAF'. This petite variety is just 18 to 20 inches tall, produces plentiful foliage, and is slow to bolt.

'BOUQUET'. This one is early flowering and compact. It's one of my favorite varieties to grow for its prolific seed production.

'MAMMOTH'. This is great for the back of the border, as it easily towers to 5 feet tall.

WHEN TO SOW Direct sow after the last frost date.

SOIL Moist, well-drained soil

PREFERRED LIGHT Full sun

Tips + Tricks

GROWING

- Companion plant with cabbage, lettuce, and onions. Keep away from carrots and tomatoes, as dill attracts hornworms.

- Direct sow in early spring as soon as the soil can be worked.

- Avoid transplanting because that can easily damage dill's delicate taproot. If you do start it indoors, sow it in a biodegradable container that can be planted directly in the ground, to avoid disturbing the roots. Or let nature do all the work. All you need is to get one dill plant established in your garden. Let that plant go to seed and it will drop dozens of volunteers that'll happily sprout next year.

- Succession sow every 2 weeks through August for a continuous supply of zesty leaves.

- Keep this gangly herb standing upright by growing it in bunches or against something that can keep it propped up in strong winds.

- Harvest dill's edible flowers from July to September and add a sprinkling of whimsy to your fish and vegetable dishes.

HARVESTING

- Begin to harvest once the plant has four or five fully established leaves.

- Pick for leaf harvest just before the flowers open. This is when the leaves contain the highest concentration of oils. Dill's flavor is best when the plant just begins to flower.

- If you allow dill to flower, leaf production will stop. Seeds ripen 2 to 3 weeks after flowering.

- Dill leaves are best eaten shortly after harvesting, so cut just what you need when you need it. Even when stored for just a few days, dill loses its zing. When dried, it loses its flavor almost completely. Frozen, it's okay at best. But when fresh, it's simply divine.

- Some varieties of dill can grow into tall, wobbly monsters that flop everywhere once seed heads get big and heavy. Ideally, it's best to wait to harvest the seeds until they ripen on the plant, but when it becomes ganglier than desired, you can harvest the seed heads just before the seeds begin to ripen, then place the seed heads upside down in a ventilated brown paper bag (use a bamboo skewer to puncture a few holes in the bag for airflow) and hang to dry. In a few weeks, as the seeds ripen, they'll collect in the bottom of the bag.

- To protect dill's delicious, delicate flavor in the kitchen, use scissors to snip it rather than chop it with a knife.

Delicious *and* Medicinal

Dill has a number of medicinal properties. It's great for the digestive system, helping to relax cramping muscles. It's a wonderful sleep aid. In fact, the name *dill* is derived from the Norse verb *dilla*, which means "to lull." And if you forgot your breath freshener, just pop a few dill seeds into your mouth and chew for sweeter breath.

LEMON VERBENA

This is probably the most fragrant plant in my garden. Anything lemon-scented smells heavenly in my opinion, but there is nothing like the sweet, lemony aromatics and taste that lemon verbena offers. One whiff of its bright, crisp scent and you'll be smitten. Sadly, lemon verbena is not a fan of cold weather, so it only grows as an annual here in Maine. The plants stay rather small, but they are full of the most delicious leaves.

WHEN TO SOW Extremely difficult to grow from seed, as not many of the seeds lemon verbena produces end up being viable, so it's best to start with a purchased plant or propagate via stem cutting.

SOIL Well-drained, compost-rich soil

PREFERRED LIGHT Full sun

Medicinal Properties

Antioxidant, anti-inflammatory, antispasmodic, antifungal

Tips + Tricks

- Shield this tender perennial from frost by providing a protective cover if temperatures dip below 32°F/0°C.

- Maximize the essential oil in this herb's leaves by providing at least 8 hours of full sun per day.

- Provide good drainage to ensure healthy plants. If their roots stay wet for long, they'll rot.

- Fertilize. In general, herbs don't need fertilizer, but lemon verbena marches to the beat of its own drummer and likes to be fed three or four times during the growing season.

- When planting in containers, choose a 12-inch-diameter pot to give the roots room to spread.

- Don't panic when you see your lemon verbena drop its leaves. When the days shorten or drop below 40°F/5°C, lemon verbena goes into dormancy. Try overwintering it by bringing it indoors; keeping it in a cool, low-light spot; and trimming back gangly stems.

- Dry the leaves on screens or hang in loose bunches or branches in a cool, dark place. Lemon verbena dries like a dream and with lightning speed.

- Store the leaves whole and crumble right before using for the best flavor.

EAT

LEMON VERBENA GRANITA

This refreshing treat is quick and simple to whip up. Blend 1 cup fresh lemon verbena leaves and 1 cup sugar in a food processor. Add ¼ cup lemon juice and pulse until well blended. Pour this mixture into 3 cups warm water and stir until the sugar has dissolved. Let steep for 15 minutes. Strain the mixture through a fine-mesh sieve and pour the liquid into a shallow dish. Cover and freeze. Scrape the mixture with a fork every 30 minutes or so for a total of four times. Scrape again right before serving.

LEMON VERBENA–INFUSED HONEY

To make 1 cup infused honey: Wash and thoroughly dry a handful of fresh lemon verbena leaves, setting aside some smaller ones. Combine the leaves, 1 cup honey, and a good grating of lemon zest from ½ lemon in a saucepan over low heat. Simmer for 10 minutes, stirring occasionally. Remove from the heat and let sit for 2 hours. Place the reserved smaller leaves in a clean, sterilized 8-ounce jar. Reheat the honey mixture slightly until warm and strain into the jar. Seal tightly. This honey should keep for up to 1 year when stored at room temperature (not that it will last that long after you try it!).

MINT

Every garden should have a pot or two of this lovely, versatile herb. It delights every sense, making even the mundane task of watering an aromatic experience.

WHEN TO SOW
Best started by cuttings rather than from seed.

SOIL
Compost-rich, moist soil

PREFERRED LIGHT Full sun; tolerates part shade

Favorite Varieties

Have fun and explore! There are so many incredible varieties to try. But make sure to keep your different varieties planted a good bit away from each other, otherwise the mints will intermingle and create a new strain with its own taste.

CHOCOLATE MINT. Though more chocolate in its aroma than taste, this mint makes for a delightful cup of tea.

MOJITO MINT. Mojito offers a subtle mint flavor. Its bright green, textured leaves look lovely in garden beds.

ORANGE MINT. Its scent is unmistakable, a mixture of citrus and bergamot.

PEPPERMINT. This packs the biggest menthol punch of all mint varieties. It's the best one to use for medicinal benefits.

Tips + Tricks

- Deter carrot flies by placing a pot of mint near carrots, parsley, and celery. Mint's strong scent also repels the white cabbage moth, so partner this herb with brassicas. Also, mint's a great pal to peas, beans, squash, and tomatoes.

- Ensure continued harvests for next year by choosing mint varieties whose hardiness is suited to overwinter in your growing zone.

- Propagate by cuttings because mint is difficult to grow from seed; it easily hybridizes between different varieties, which means that what germinates may not be true to type of the parent plant.

- Keep your containers well watered. This thirsty herb isn't a fan of dry soil and may need watering twice daily during heat spells.

- Stop the spread before it begins. Mint reproduces underground via rhizomes and can become invasive. Help corral its growth by planting it in a container or putting it into a bottomless container buried in the garden bed.

- Harvest mint right before it flowers. This is when its essential oil content is at its highest, allowing for maximum flavor and medicinal properties.

- Pinch the stems back to the first set of leaves when harvesting to encourage bushiness.

- Avoid letting mint go to flower if you plan on using its leaves. Once in flower, the herb stops producing the essential oils that are responsible for its fabulous flavor.

Mint's Medicinal Properties

Most of mint's valuable medicinal magic lies in its menthol, the main constituent of its volatile oil. Menthol is also to credit for mint's rejuvenating aroma. As a medicinal herb, mint is antibacterial, antispasmodic, antimicrobial, analgesic, a stimulant, and a nervine.

MINT-ROSEMARY CLEANSING GRAINS

The herbal combination of rosemary and mint has always been my personal go-to, but the way my face looks and feels each morning after using these cleansing grains is unbelievable. Not only does it make skin glow bright, but the mint's menthol also stimulates blood flow, sending a happy zesty feeling across the cheeks.

MAKES FIVE 4-OUNCE BOTTLES

- 4 ounces colloidal oats (ground oats)
- 4 ounces kaolin clay
- 2 ounces almond meal
- ½ ounce powdered honey
- ¼ ounce dried rosemary, ground
- ¼ ounce dried mint, ground
- ½ ounce baking soda
- 12 drops rosemary essential oil
- 10 drops peppermint essential oil

1 Mix together the oats, kaolin, almond meal, powdered honey, rosemary, and mint in a large bowl.

2 Put the baking soda in a small bowl. Add the essential oils and thoroughly incorporate (this will evenly distribute the essential oils throughout the cleansing grains). Add the baking soda mixture to the oats mixture and stir to combine.

Store the mixture in glass jars or containers.

TO USE: Pour a tablespoon of cleansing grains in your hand. Drizzle in enough water to make a paste that is fluid enough to be applied to your face like a mask. Gently apply across your entire face, avoiding the eye area. Let the cleansing grains dry on your face for 3 to 5 minutes; as the paste dries, it takes on a green hue. Using a warm cloth, gently wash off the paste. Finish with a few splashes of cold water.

MINT SUNBURN SOOTHER

The next time a little too much fun in the sun leaves you feeling burned, go out to your mint patch for some soothing relief in a pinch. Grab a handful of mint and brew up a strong cup of tea, but wait— don't drink it. Instead, pop it in the fridge for a few hours, then gently apply the liquid with a cotton pad to burned areas. Menthol's cooling properties will provide much-needed soothing and relief.

Mint Sugar

Sprinkle on fruit salads, rim a cocktail glass with some, or stir into iced teas and lemonades; as many mints as there are, there's a dish certain to benefit from the sweetness that is mint-infused sugar.

There are two methods to prepare the infused sugar: One is a layered method, the other is blended in a food processor.

Layering leaves. Wash the mint leaves and dry them well. Spread a layer of granulated sugar in a mason jar. Top with a layer of fresh mint leaves, then apply a granulated sugar layer. Repeat until the layers reach an inch below the rim. Cover tightly and store for 1 month. During this time, the sugar infuses with the mint leaves. Sprinkle the infused sugar in teas, on fruit salads, or on top of baked goods. You can even nosh on the dried mint leaves as an added treat.

Blended beauty. Preparing mint sugar in a food processor not only makes for a delicious treat for the belly, it also blends up to a beautiful pale green hue. Combine ¾ cup granulated sugar with ½ cup fresh mint leaves in a food processor; pulse until the mixture is well blended. Use immediately or, for longer storage, spread in a single layer on a baking sheet, let air-dry overnight, then store in a small jar.

MINT EXTRACT

Think about how much tastier that peppermint fudge will be with your own garden-fresh extract. Take a handful of mint. Rinse and pat dry. Remove the leaves and give them a good smash to release their oils. Place in a mason jar and cover completely with vodka—the cheap stuff will do. Cover with a lid. Set aside in a cool, dark place and give the jar a good weekly shake. In about 6 weeks, give the extract a taste test. If it's minty enough for you, strain, bottle, and use as you would store-bought mint extract. If you'd like a bit more kick, strain out the old mint leaves and replace with fresh, then let it sit for a few more weeks. It should be mint-licious.

SUMMER

THYME

Each summer, I look forward to my thyme hedging, planted en masse with sweet alyssum. There's an undeniable charm about this beloved herb, whose magic goes well beyond the kitchen—thyme is pure herbal skin magic, too. It's been said that Ancient Greeks sprinkled thyme in their baths and medieval knights carried pieces of embroidered thyme on them as a symbol of courage. With a history like that, it's pretty cool to have it humbly growing in the garden outside your door.

WHEN TO SOW Start indoors 6 to 8 weeks before the last frost date, barely covering the seed. Germination can be slow at first, then it takes off.

SOIL Sandy, dry soil; root rot can develop in wet soil

PREFERRED LIGHT Full sun

Medicinal Properties

Antioxidant, antibacterial, antispasmodic, anti-inflammatory, antiseptic, antimicrobial, carminative

Favorite Varieties

Different varieties of thyme are hardier to certain zones. German, winter, and English thyme are great perennials for Zones 5 to 9, but French and lemon thyme aren't as hardy and are better grown as annuals outside of Zones 7 to 9.

Tips + Tricks

GROWING

◆ Companion plant with brassicas, tomatoes, and strawberries. Thyme is a foe to cabbageworms, hornworms, and flea beetles.

◆ Avoid overwatering, as this herb does not tolerate wet soil.

◆ Allow the soil to go completely dry between watering, then give it a good soaking.

◆ Trim frequently to encourage plants to produce new growth.

HARVESTING

◆ Harvest in the morning just after the dew dries.

◆ Harvest before the herb begins to flower. Once it flowers, the herb's essential oil production dries up and the leaves lose their flavor or become bitter.

◆ Stop harvesting 1 month before the first frost date to allow the plant time to harden off before the cold of winter.

Magical Thymol

Thymol, the chief chemical constituent of thyme, is the heart of this herb's magic. Thymol is a powerful disinfectant used in everything from mouthwashes and skin care to household cleaning disinfectants and pest repellants.

NOURISH

THYME–APPLE CIDER VINEGAR TONER

Give some dried thyme a good crushing to help release its volatile oils. Fill a clean jar three-quarters full with the crushed thyme. Mix one part apple cider vinegar to two parts water in a measuring cup, then pour over the thyme up to the top inch of the jar. Seal the jar with a plastic or other non-reactive lid and place in the refrigerator. Let the mixture infuse for 2 weeks, giving the jar a gentle shake occasionally. Strain out the solids through cheesecloth and jar the liquid. Keep stored in the refrigerator. To use, apply toner to your face with cotton balls or a soft cloth after cleansing.

Herbs for Chickens in & out of the Coop

Mint. Plant a border of mint around the outside of your coop to ward off mice. Add a handful to some cold water in summer to give your birds a cool, quenching treat.

Lavender. Spruce up nesting boxes with a sprinkle of lavender leaves and flowers and gift your hens a little bit of calm. Lavender's strong scent helps repel insects.

Calendula. Add this herb to nesting boxes. Or toss some petals into their feed to give yolks a little extra beta-carotene and a brighter orange hue.

Parsley. Grab a bunch of fresh stems for a nutritious, quick chicken snack chock-full of vitamins, iron, calcium, and zinc.

Thyme. Hang in bunches to promote respiratory health or mix with some mint and water in the summer for a cooling infusion rich in antioxidants.

Oregano. Add a sprig or two to the waterer for an infusion of oregano's antibacterial goodness, or sprinkle a handful of crushed dried oregano into the birds' food.

Favorite Summer Flowers

Summer's flowers are not shy about making their presence known. Bright hues of vivid oranges, yellows, pinks, purples, and blue roll across the garden landscape, transforming it into a patchwork of petals in every shape, texture, and height.

Cosmos

🌼 I can't imagine my garden without the charm and cheer of cosmos. Whether it be the tried-and-true 'Sensation Mix', the captivating 'Cupcakes and Saucers', or the orange loveliness that is 'Bright Lights', there's a variety of cosmos out there just waiting for your garden.

🌼 Loves full sun and isn't fussy about its soil.

🌼 Is a fast bloomer. Flowers open as early as 3 months from sowing.

🌼 Don't sow until 4 to 5 weeks before the last frost date, as smaller cosmos plants experience less transplant shock. And make sure to wait until your soil is warmed to transplant cosmos into the garden: The plant will be unhappy in chilly soil, especially chilly, wet soil.

🌼 Encourage bushier plants (which means more flowers) by keeping the plants pinched back, starting at seedling stage. When seedlings reach 8 to 10 inches tall, pinch back to right above the first set of true leaves.

🌼 Keep blooms going all the way through frost by doing a second sowing a month after the initial sowing.

🌼 Keep deadheading for nonstop flowers all season long.

🌼 Create a garden display that pops by partnering cosmos with anise hyssop, calendula, dahlias, nicotiana, zinnias, and cleome.

🌼 Cosmos is pollinator-friendly, drought resistant, and an active self-seeder.

Petunia

- 🌼 Likes full sun and compost-rich, moist, well-drained soil.

- 🌼 Comes in two growing habits: compact and bushy or trailing.

- 🌼 Reliably produces prolific color all season long.

- 🌼 Grows well in containers.

- 🌼 Sow seed 8 to 10 weeks before the last frost date. Petunias are slow to start from seed, but the seedlings catch up fast.

- 🌼 Do not cover the seeds with soil; they need light to germinate.

- 🌼 Deadhead often for prolonged blooms.

- 🌼 Prune back the trailing varieties to prevent them from becoming straggly.

Foxglove

- 🌼 This cool-weather flower enjoys full sun but tolerates part shade.

- 🌼 Plant in compost-rich, well-drained soil.

- 🌼 Most foxgloves are short-lived perennials.

- 🌼 Often doesn't flower until its second year. Get blooms in the first year by growing my favorite variety, 'Foxy', a wonderful annual that provides a beautiful bouquet of blooms.

- 🌼 Encourage a second flush of blooms by cutting back after the first flowers finish.

- 🌼 Save seeds for next year by collecting their easy-to-gather seedpods, or leave some behind on the soil to allow this active self-seeder to spread.

- 🌼 Do not eat any part of the plant; foxglove is toxic.

Geraniums

🌼 Prefer full sun but tolerate part shade in compost-rich, well-drained soil.

🌼 Easy to start from seed or by cuttings.

🌼 Bring indoors to overwinter and be rewarded with a beautiful houseplant that will produce flowers year-round. Once the warm weather rolls back around, you can return the plant to the garden to bask in another season of sun.

🌼 Explore scented geraniums. They are an absolute joy to grow, and you'll delight in their intoxicating aromatics. Varieties include citronella, pineapple, rose, chocolate, and apple.

🌼 Avoid fertilizing, as that dulls the scent of this wonderful plant.

Impatiens

🌼 Plant this quick-growing, low-maintenance annual in partial sun to shade in rich, well-drained soil.

🌼 Blooms spring through frost.

🌼 Thrives in containers.

🌼 Be sure they receive a good 2-inch drink of water a week, as impatiens dislike drying out.

🌼 Avoid downy mildew by growing the New Guinea varieties, which are resistant to it.

🌼 When your impatiens seedpods are big and fat, give them a light touch and watch each pod burst open and spray its seeds everywhere.

🌼 Check out the double impatiens varieties if you're like me and love the idea of roses but don't currently grow any. The doubles look like a carpet of petite roses and are especially charming when planted with hosta, coleus, balsam, and bleeding hearts in a shade garden.

Cleome

🌸 Enjoys full sun to part shade and compost-rich, well-drained soil.

🌸 Encourage better germination by patting seeds onto the soil when sowing; they need light to germinate.

🌸 Drought tolerant.

🌸 Cleome's sweet nectar attracts butterflies, hummingbirds, and other pollinators.

🌸 Provide a midseason feeding of fertilizer to encourage growth for the rest of the season.

🌸 Create a little garden awe by growing cleome as a back-of-the-garden border plant. Incorporate some zinnias and cosmos for an especially striking combination.

🌸 A word of warning: The fragrance of these plants is, well, more like Eau du Skunk than something floral.

Globe Gilia

🌸 Enjoys full sun to part shade in compost-rich, well-drained soil.

🌸 Direct sow 2 to 3 weeks before your last frost date.

🌸 The seeds need light to germinate and can be slow to sprout.

🌸 The bee's knees of blooms. Bees flock by the dozens to feast in the nectar-rich blossoms. Attracts butterflies and hummingbirds, too.

🌸 Sow every 2 weeks for season-long blooms.

Love-in-a-Mist

🌸 Likes full sun but tolerates some shade. Prefers well-drained, compost-rich soil.

🌸 Cover seeds very lightly with vermiculite after sowing.

🌸 Doesn't like transplanting, so best to direct sow in early spring.

🌸 Enjoys cooler weather.

🌸 Succession sow every few weeks for season-long blooms.

🌸 Works better as a front-of-the-border plant.

🌸 Favorite varieties include 'Persian Jewels' and 'Miss Jekyll'.

🌸 Seed heads make stunning dried botanicals.

🌸 Is deer resistant and an active self-seeder.

Foraging from Nature's Summer Garden

Foraging isn't just an occasional adventure—after a while, it becomes a seasonal tradition. Although I start scouting my locations a few times prior to collecting, the plants are remarkably predictable in their timing. Without fail, the last week of June brings endless elderflowers in one location, but I have to wait 2 more weeks until they're ready for picking in another. In some years, keeping a close eye on the rugosa roses coming into bloom can mean the difference between gathering basketfuls or handfuls. While it's easy to think foraging is as simple as hopping out and grabbing some wild goodies, your success at bringing home a heaping harvest depends on the observation and legwork you do before heading out to harvest, to ensure that your foraging delights will be waiting for you when you arrive.

Elderflowers

My hunt for elderberries led me to discover my deeper love for elderflowers and their heavenly, honey-scented blooms. My quest for elderberries was truly my maiden voyage in foraging for a new-to-me plant. Previously, I had foraged only familiar items I could safely identify. So I studied up on American elder and what to look for to identify the shrub. I felt fairly confident that I'd know it as soon as I saw it. So out I went to a spot down the road by a river and exploded with glee when I saw that umbrella of deep purple berries. I clipped away and joyfully returned home with a big basket of berries. I also took a few clippings of leaves and stems to ensure proper identification before eating.

Back home, the first thing I did was consult the American elder monograph to confirm my berries' identification. My glee melted into gloom. My basket did not contain elderberries but berries of a plant called devil's walking stick. Just by that name alone, it pretty much says "Don't eat me." Into the compost went my forage findings. But what a valuable lesson I gained. Before I'd head out again, I needed to really study up. So that's what I did the following winter.

Come early the next summer, I had worked out a plan to up my ID game: A good way to improve elderberry identification skill is to visit the foraging locations when the plant is in bloom. Seeing the flowers helps confirm the plant's ID, then you can return a few months later when the flowers have been replaced by purple jeweled orbs.

My quest for elderflowers began to diminish when I struggled to find any plants. A lot of similar shrubs, yes, but no elder. Then, as I was walking along the perimeter of a field, I spotted a hidden tunnel of green. Of course, I entered it, and what I came upon still feels a bit storybook to recount. The tunnel led to an open circle of grass bordered all around by huge, old American elders. I could not believe my eyes. At last, I found my herbal pot of gold.

ELDERFLOWER & ROSE MILK BATH

Elderflowers are all sorts of yummy for your skin—especially maturing skin. They help reduce fine lines and wrinkles, promote new cell growth, minimize pore size, and more. So treat yourself with a soak in this bath of queens (Cleopatra was a fan of milk baths).

MAKES 32 OUNCES

- 2 cups dry milk powder
- 1 cup oat flour
- ¼ cup Epsom salts
- ¼ cup baking soda
- ⅛ cup cornstarch
- 1 tablespoon powdered dried elderflowers
- 1 tablespoon powdered dried rose petals
- 1 tablespoon ground dried orange peel

Stir together the ingredients in a large bowl until well combined. Store in a glass container in a cool spot out of direct sun.

TO USE: Draw a tub of warm water. Right before you step into the tub, shake 2 to 4 tablespoons of the mixture into the running water. Take a deep breath and enjoy the burst of aromatherapy while your skin soaks in the silky goodness.

Nettles

I discovered we had nettles in the most unfortunate of ways—I fell on some. At first, I
assumed I had disturbed a nest of ground bees, the sting was that bad. I seriously never
thought a plant could be responsible for this pain . . . but it was. Known as stinging
nettle (which I concur is a very apt title), this perennial is quite the Swiss Army knife of
herbs—you can eat it, drink it, use it medicinally, and make an incredible fertilizer and
compost activator from it. You can even harvest fibers from the stalk. But how do you do
that if the darn plant bites back? Thankfully, once dried, nettle loses its sting. That sting,
by the way, is caused by a histamine contained in the tiny hairs that cover the plant. It's
been said that jewelweed, sage, or rosemary rubbed on the irritated area helps
ease the reaction.

The good news is that if you have nettle growing about, it
means that you also have happy, rich soil, because that's
what it loves to grow in. Spring is a great time to
pinch back nettle plants (wearing gloves!) to
encourage them to grow bushier.

Ways to Use Nettle

- Dry some for tea.

- Use the leaves fresh as a swap for spinach. Nettle is full of good nutritional components like calcium, iron, chlorophyll, and vitamins A and C.

- Come fall, collect those nettle seeds and sprinkle them on your oatmeal, on salads, or in muffins and breads for another great nutritional boost.

- Fresh nettle boiled for 15 minutes, then cooled, strained, and combined with a splash of apple cider vinegar makes for a good hair conditioner.

GROW

NETTLE TEA GARDEN FERTILIZER

Feed your plants a buffet of nitrogen, potassium, iron, and more with nettle tea fertilizer. With your gloves on, head out and collect a bunch of nettles. Cut the leafy stalks into chunks and drop into a large bucket. Fill with enough water to cover the nettles by an inch or two. To keep the nettles submerged, place a rock or weight on top of them. Set the bucket aside, and in 1 month you'll have garden gold ready to get your plants growing.

To use: Strain and then dilute the nettle tea with water in a 1:10 ratio.

Roses

Considering that rugosa roses are on the invasive species list in Maine, it's easily said that we have a lot of roses here to forage. These beautiful wild roses grow along beaches and roads and burst with the perfect punch of rose essence. Historically, damask and cabbage rose varieties were used to make rose water, thanks to their heavy perfumed scent. Some of today's rose hybrids are gorgeous but lack an aroma, so they would not be good choices for making rose water. Rather, look for old-fashioned varieties, as they tend to have the strongest fragrance. But as long as any rose offers some sort of scent, you can make a floral water. Just keep in mind that you'll need to infuse a larger quantity of subtle-scented petals to bring the maximum fragrance to the water.

Remember to Go Back for Rose Hips

Take note of your favorite rose-petal-foraging haunts early in summer, for you'll want to return come late summer to pick some rose hips. From August through early fall, rose hips ripen and are ready for harvest (though they sweeten after a little frost). Be sure to leave plenty on the plant for your bird pals!

◆ Rose hips are chock-full of vitamin C.

◆ When picking, go for scent over looks. Select firm, vibrant hips.

◆ Use in tea, syrups, and jellies. For tea, spoon 1 teaspoon dried hips into 1 cup hot water.

◆ When drying large rose hips like those from *Rosa rugosa*, cut the hips in half and remove the seeds before drying the flesh for tea.

NOURISH

ROSE WATER

This pretty potion can be used in everything from body care to cooking and cocktails. You can even make a room or linen spray out of it. Add it to lotions, baths, cooling mists, even shampoos. My favorite is to use it as a wetting agent for my dried cleansing grains (see page 108). I also apply it as a toner (add a splash of witch hazel for extra toning goodness). And feel free to swap out the roses for other favorite flowers like violas, lavender, chamomile, geranium, or rosemary.

Gently rinse the petals to rid them of any dirt and bugs. Place the petals in a heatproof bowl. Boil a kettle of distilled water and pour enough water over the petals to just cover them completely. Let the petals infuse until their color has faded, 12 to 24 hours. Strain through cheesecloth into a clean jar, making sure to squeeze out every last drop of liquid from the petals. Keep in the refrigerator for 1 to 2 weeks. You can add vodka or witch hazel as a preservative to extend the rose water's shelf life, if desired, though I tend to make mine in small batches and use it fresh.

Autumn

A Time to Reflect

Autumn here in New England is like nothing else. Summer's bright landscape ebbs into rich, deep jewel tones that build up to a spectacular show of color extending from land to sky. A familiar crispness fills the air, and as animals and birds begin to prep for the colder days ahead, you realize it's time for you to do the same.

The frantic pace of summer begins to slow, allowing you pockets of time to continue relishing the riches in front of you even as you reflect upon the growing journey you had this year. Of course, while you're both savoring the moment and looking at the past, you're also giddy with excitement for what next year's garden could bring. And the anticipation of a whole new growing season begins.

Garden Cleanup

Who knew the key to great garden cleanup is doing less and getting a whole lot more? Prepping your garden for a proper winter slumber truly is key to kicking off your spring with success. What you do now will affect the impact that some pests and disease can have. Plus, all prep done now sets you up for a jump start on spring sowings.

Here are a few tips for tucking in your garden for the season.

❋ Most of your garden plants can be composted, but be careful to remove all diseased or infected plant materials by bagging up and disposing of them.

❋ As tempting as it is to cut down spent perennials and flower heads, leave them standing for fall and winter and cut them down come spring. The seed heads provide a valuable food source for your bird friends, and the stems offer shelter to many beneficial insects.

❋ Rather than pull out pea and bean plants from the ground, cut them just above ground level instead. That way, you leave those precious feeding roots in the soil to continue to release their nitrogen goodness.

❋ Gather bamboo poles and terra-cotta pots and store them in an area sheltered from the weather and extreme cold.

❋ Apply a heaping helping of compost to the top of each bed—I usually add 8 to 12 inches.

❋ Top-dress your beds with shredded leaves or other organic matter to help feed the soil.

TO TILL OR NOT TO TILL

No-till gardening worked beautifully for me for over a decade, until one year when I paid a rather hefty price and learned a valuable lesson. Each spring for several years, I would simply cultivate the first few inches of soil using my fingers to loosen it up, then I would add a good helping of compost on top. I religiously practiced crop rotation as well. This practice worked for me without any issues, only benefits.

But one spring, I suffered the worst crop loss in my decades of gardening—because of a vile creature called the cabbage-root maggot. It decimated every single crop in the brassica family, taking out one-third of my garden. I learned that this maggot's pupa overwinters in the top 5 inches of soil. It even survives Maine winters, which really shows its hardiness. The best method to control any emerging population is to till the soil both in fall (burying the puparium) and again come spring (to deter eggs from emerging). The pesky carrot-rust fly also overwinters this way, but in the top 3 inches of soil.

So should you till or not? Like everything in the garden, it's a balance. I hand till only when I think it's really needed for certain beds—such as in the case of cabbage-root maggots. Otherwise, it's best to not disturb the soil, because the structure of and nutrients in those top inches are important to healthy soil and happy plants.

Hügel Beds

My garden cleanup creates the foundation materials for new garden beds. They're called hügelkultur beds—no-dig, layered garden beds that slowly release nutrients from decomposing plant material into the soil below. The wood and branches at the base of the bed retain and slowly release water back into the soil. Because of this, these beds fare well during times when rainfall is scarce. The layers of bed materials also create great structure for plant roots to stretch out in. And if you're squeezed for gardening space, build up the soil so that it mounds in the center of the bed, almost shaping it into an arch. By mounding in this manner, you're creating more soil surface area and thus additional growing space.

Hügelkultur beds are truly a win-win all around, because they are constructed with woodland, yard, and kitchen waste. It's the ultimate recycling that yields rich soil that makes plants happy.

Build Your Own Hügelkultur Beds

1. Collect yard waste such as rotting logs, leaves, twigs, branches, grass, straw, and plants.

2. Place a layer of damp cardboard or newspaper over the area where your new bed will be. This will smother the weeds below.

3. Add a layer of logs, branches, and twigs.

4. Spread a heaping layer of leaves, grass clippings, straw, and other herbaceous plant material.

5. Shovel on a 12-inch layer of topsoil.

6. Top with a 12-inch layer of compost.

7. Let settle for several weeks. (Whenever possible, I let my beds overwinter for one season before planting so the beds can settle fully.) During this period, you'll notice that some topsoil and compost shift as they fill in gaps between the branches, logs, and other plant material. Because of this, you may need to add a second topping of compost prior to planting. As the materials break down over the years and the bed settles, you'll want to continue to add a good top dressing of compost to the bed each spring.

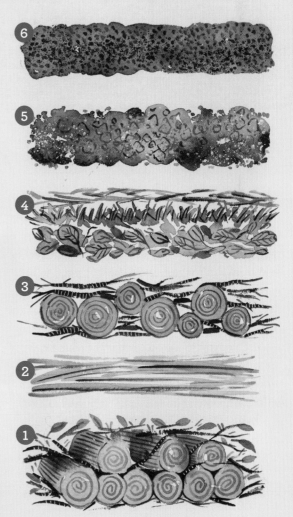

Soil Microbiomes & the Soul

There's a whole lot of magic being made in the top few inches of your soil. Out of eyesight, plant roots symbiotically play with microscopic organisms, and together they work toward creating an optimal environment for your plant and you. A great example of happy soil-plant partners are legumes like peas and favas and a soil bacteria called rhizobia. The rhizobia attach to a legume's roots and help capture or "fix" nitrogen that the plant can use to grow. As a good partner, the plant returns the favor by creating a larger, more bountiful root system that benefits the soil bacteria. Growing legumes ultimately boosts the nitrogen levels in your soil, which is extremely helpful when looking to plant in a bed that previously hosted heavy feeders like tomatoes or strawberries.

Ever have your garden beds invaded by mushrooms? Turns out, those mushrooms might be great helpers. Fungi in soil help plant's roots take in vital nutrients like phosphorus and zinc, which are needed to create chlorophyll. In return, the soil repays the favor by secreting the glucose created by chlorophyll back into the soil where the hungry fungi happily feed on it.

Just like trees have their own language and communicate across forests via their root system, soil microbiomes communicate in a similar fashion when a predator is present. A vast web of fungus, called mycorrhizae, carries communications between plants. This system warns nearby plants of predators, signaling natural defenses to help repel invaders.

These examples just scratch the surface in terms of explaining how rich soil truly is the key to successful growing and creating a healthy environment. There's a lot more information to dig deep into and learn from.

Reflections at the End of the Season

Remember that garden journal you swore last winter you'd keep meticulous notes in? If you fell off the journaling wagon over the busy growing season, right now is a great time to dig out your notebook and quickly jot down some observations from the past growing season. You don't have go into detail—just capture enough information that, come the slower days of winter, you can flesh out your notes. It's easy to swear that you'll remember something or promise yourself that you'll jot down your observations later, but often it just doesn't happen. I've learned this lesson over too many years of not writing things down when I thought of them. Let's just say reflecting now will prove priceless later.

Here are a few tips for creating healthy, happy soil.

❋ Cultivate a microbiome by building up the soil in the same beds and maintaining the same paths around them.

❋ Add a good helping of compost each spring.

❋ Avoid tilling, if possible.

❋ Plant cover crops—that is, crops that help feed the soil—in fall especially after growing heavy feeders like tomatoes.

❋ Encourage diversity—it matters! Planting a combination of vegetables, herbs, and flowers together in the same beds not only creates a dynamic visual environment but also boosts the variety of soil-benefiting microbes that in turn make available a wider range of nutrients.

Birds in Need

When you plot out your garden, consider how it can help feed and nourish resident and migrating birds. Bird populations across the globe are on the decline, but it is so easy—and so very rewarding—to become a bird steward.

Being with my bird pals in the garden is one of my favorite things. Come July, when the garden has become a jungle of vines, trellises, and archways, birds of all kinds flock in to hang, hide, feed, and nest throughout the garden. The goldfinches feed on the sunflowers in droves. Yellow warblers tuck themselves inside the broccoli and kale plants, noshing on cabbageworms. Hummingbirds spend the day zipping and zooming among the scarlet runner beans. I've watched chipping sparrows raise their young at the base of the wild raspberry border and robin babes take their first flight from the nest to a trellis full of morning glories. I take it as the biggest compliment to have their company. To bear witness to such intimate corners of their lives . . . well, no words seem fitting to explain that kind of magic. The garden is theirs now, and I'm just a thankful visitor.

MAKE

Make Your Own Suet

Mix 3½ cups sunflower seeds or wild bird seed mix, 1 cup quick oats, and ½ cup cornmeal in a large bowl. Melt 1½ cups coconut oil and ¾ cup crunchy peanut butter in a microwavable bowl. Stir well, then pour the peanut butter mixture into the seed mixture. Scoop the suet into ice cube trays or molds of your choice and freeze until solid.

Fabulous Garden Cleanup Helpers

While my feathery friends are banned from free ranging in the garden during the growing season, I happily allow them to run amok this time of year, because chickens are some of the best garden janitors you can have.

- Henny pennies will nip away any remaining veggies and herbs. (But keep them away from plants in the nightshade family, such as tomatoes and eggplant, as those plants contain a toxin called solanine.)

- Chickens will eat weed seeds.

- Chickens aerate the soil with their scratching, as they rid the beds of grubs and other bad bugs. Many of the insects that cause so much garden heartbreak overwinter in the top few inches of soil. The hens help not only by eating the grubs, reducing future bad bug populations, but by disturbing the top layer of soil, literally pushing larvae out of their comfort zone.

- They'll fluff up and spread out mulch and leaves.

- They'll add their own layer of compost. Chicken manure is chock-full of good growing material and adds nitrogen to the soil. By the time spring rolls around, the manure will have aged enough to be beneficial to the plants. (Fresh manure can be too much of a good thing—it can burn plants.)

- Before you let your flock free, however, fence off any areas where you don't want their help (such as that patch of lettuce that's still cranking). And be a protective mother hen—don't leave chickens unattended while they're free ranging! In our area, we have an active hawk population, along with other predators like foxes, weasels, and raccoons; our best defense is sheer attentiveness.

Gardening in Stolen Moments

My reality, and I can only imagine it's true for so many others, is that my garden is grown in stolen moments. Juggling life's other responsibilities often leaves weekends as the only time to work in the garden. And when you look at all the tending and chores that need to get accomplished during that weekend, gardening can easily become overwhelming, and your garden will feel more like a chore than nourishment.

The truth is that those little minutes you take throughout your day all add up. You walk the dog through the garden, pulling up a few weeds along the way. Or during your after-work harvest scramble, you gather enough for dinner and for preserving as well. Or in my case, as I walk to the coop to let the hens into their run, I stop to sow a row in the early morning. These little stolen moments make a big difference. So rather than saving that long list of to-dos for the weekend, tack it on the fridge and try to sneak in a few tasks throughout the week. That way, you'll have time in your weekend for soaking in the joy of your garden, not slaving in it.

GARLIC

Once you've had your own garden-fresh garlic, nothing store-bought can compare. And once you start growing it, with each passing season you'll feel the urge to plant more . . . and more . . . and more! What I adore about garlic is that it's almost a "plant it and forget it" kind of crop. Plus, you plant it in fall, skirting the manic spring rush. And if you plant hardneck varieties, you'll get a bonus: delicious flower stalks called garlic scapes in spring.

WHEN TO SOW
Plant bulbs in fall, about 5 weeks after first fall frost. (Here in Zone 5, we plant ours in mid- to late October.)

SOIL Compost-rich, well-drained soil

PREFERRED LIGHT
Full sun

Favorite Varieties

I prefer growing hardneck varieties because I covet scapes. My go-to varieties include 'Chesnok Red', 'German Red', 'Music', 'German Extra Hardy', and 'Russian Red'.

Tips + Tricks

◆ Plant garlic in the first 5 weeks after your first fall frost date. Ideally, you don't want the garlic to sprout—only develop a good root system, so best to not plant too early. Select a sunny spot with a bed full of rich compost and good drainage. Sow individual cloves, root end down, 6 inches apart. Push the cloves down into the soil 2 to 3 inches. Top with 4 inches of mulch like shredded leaves or straw. Wait until spring. Do a happy dance upon spying the first sprout.

◆ Provide this hungry bulb with a feeding of fish emulsion once in early spring and a second time just when the bulb begins to swell, usually mid-May in my garden. Avoid feeding after that, as too much fertilizer may stunt bulb development.

◆ Order your seed garlic by mid- to late summer to ensure you'll have it in time for planting in mid-October or early November. The planting sweet spot is just as the leaves are changing but before hard freezes arrive.

◆ Seek out high-quality organic seed stock. If you're looking for seed garlic but are not having luck finding it through traditional sellers, you can try planting store-bought garlic. Ideally, purchase unbleached stock from a local farm. Garlic sold in supermarkets often has been bleached to make the bulb more visually appealing. While this garlic will sprout when planted, because of the exposure to bleach, it may not form a quality bulb.

Harvest Tips

◆ There's an ideal window of time to harvest your garlic. Harvest too soon, and you get petite bulbs with too thin a paper wrap. Harvest too late, and the bulbs start to break open, compromising their storage life.

◆ Check your plants frequently. When you see that the bottom half of the leaves have yellowed and died back, it's time to get digging.

◆ For best storage, reduce the watering of your hardneck plants 2 to 3 weeks after removing the scapes. Too much water at this point can shorten the garlic's storage life by causing the bulb to rot and the leaves to yellow.

◆ Harvest during a dry spell, withholding water the week of digging, if possible.

◆ After harvesting, cure the bulbs. Keeping all the roots and leaves intact, lay out the garlic on a rack or screen, or hang in a shady, well-ventilated spot.

◆ After a few weeks, once the roots have shriveled and the leaves are completely dry, start cleaning the bulbs for storage. Trim off the leaves and roots and brush off the dirt.

◆ Set aside the biggest, healthiest bulbs to use for next year's seed crop.

◆ Store the remaining bulbs in a breathable container in a cool, dark place.

Elephant garlic

(*Allium ampeloprasum* var. *ampeloprasum*), botanically speaking, is not a true garlic plant; it's more closely related to leeks. Because of that, it tastes different than true garlic. Elephant garlic has a milder, oniony flavor that sometimes is best suited for use as a vegetable rather than as an herb.

Garlic Scapes

Scapes are the garlic's flower stalk. They shoot up from the leaves in midspring and then curl over. Nip off these shoots to redirect the plant's energy into forming a big, fat bulb. As a reward, you get to feast on one of the tastiest garden delights ever. Scapes taste like a garlicky green bean mixed with asparagus. Sautéed in a little olive oil with garlic and sea salt, they are pure happiness. The feasting possibilities are endless: roasted scapes, char-grilled scapes, pickled scapes, pasta with sautéed scapes, scape risotto, scape and goat cheese tart . . .

Scapes store like a dream in the refrigerator. Keep them in a plastic bag and they'll stay fresh for 2 to 3 weeks. Or keep them on your counter in a jar of water for a few days, making sure to change the water daily.

Hardneck vs. Softneck

The "neck" refers to the stem of the garlic. Softneck garlic stems flop over before harvest and are easy to braid for hanging. Hardneck varieties have stiff stems and produce garlic scapes that should be removed before they flower. Hardneck varieties tend to be easier to peel.

GARLIC SOUP

The cure for what ails you, even if that ailment is just a relentless ache for garlic soup. This mild-looking clear broth is packed with such a punch of flavor and bite that it just might knock you out of your seat. It'll knock any sickness out of you. And it will most definitely ward off any pesky vampires hanging about.

SERVES 8

- 8 cups chicken or vegetable stock
- 1 cup dry white wine
- 27 garlic cloves, peeled and halved
  Pinch of red pepper flakes
  Salt and freshly ground black pepper
- 1 tablespoon olive oil
- 1 baguette, thinly sliced
  Asiago cheese

Combine the stock, wine, 25 of the garlic cloves, and the pepper flakes in a soup pot. Bring to a boil, reduce the heat, and simmer, covered, until the garlic is soft, about 1 hour. Strain the broth through a sieve. Season with salt and pepper.

Heat the oil in a skillet over medium-high heat until it's shimmering but not smoking. Add a few baguette slices at a time and lightly brown both sides. Using the remaining 2 garlic cloves, rub each slice of toasted bread a few times.

To serve, pour the soup into individual bowls. Float a few baguette slices in each bowl and top with a healthy grating of cheese.

GARLIC SCAPE PESTO

- 2 cups fresh parsley
- 20 garlic scapes, diced
- ½ cup walnuts
- ⅓ cup grated Parmesan cheese
- ⅓ cup olive oil
  Juice of ½ lemon
  Salt and freshly ground black pepper

Chop the parsley, then combine with the scapes, nuts, and Parmesan in a food processor. Pulse until finely chopped. With the processor running, slowly pour in the oil until the desired consistency is reached. Add the lemon juice, then season with salt and pepper. Pulse a few more times, then enjoy.

MAKE YOUR OWN GARLIC POWDER

After peeling your garlic, remove the green germ that's forming inside each clove. That little thing adds bitterness, so best to remove it prior to cooking or preserving. Thinly slice each clove and place the slices in a dehydrator for a couple of hours. (Bonus: Your entire house will smell like garlic bread.) Once cracker-dry, jar up the slices. Whenever you need garlic powder, take out a few pieces and grind them in a spice grinder.

GARLIC OIL

Smash and peel 1 head of garlic. Place it along with 1 cup extra-virgin olive oil in a small saucepan and heat over medium-low heat until bubbles form around the garlic, about 3 minutes. Let simmer for 10 minutes, reducing the heat to low if the garlic begins to brown. Remove from the heat and let cool to room temperature. Store in an airtight container in the refrigerator for 1 week. Use in marinades and dressings or toss with some chopped fresh herbs for a yummy bread dip.

AUTUMN

139

TOMATOES

I love, love, love fresh garden tomatoes. Turns out, I'm not the only one—93 percent of us gardeners in the US grow tomatoes. Given that there are more than 10,000 varieties of this beloved garden gem, your head may spin with all the possible ones to grow.

WHEN TO SOW Start seeds 6 to 8 weeks before the last frost date. Transplant into the garden once the soil and temperatures have warmed, usually 4 weeks past the last frost date.

SOIL Well-drained, compost-rich soil

PREFERRED LIGHT Full sun for at least 8 hours a day

Favorite Varieties

When selecting which variety will work best for you, decide first what you're looking for in a tomato. Tomato varieties fall into three main categories: cherry, slicing, and paste.

CHERRY TOMATOES. These little garden delights can be round, pear-shaped or teardrop-shaped. They tend to be the first tomatoes to ripen and are usually one of the last to finish in autumn. Their sweet flavor is fabulous in salads and snacks and for general noshing. Favorites include 'Sungold', the 'Bumble Bee' series, and 'Super Sweet 100'.

SLICING TOMATOES. We all dream about these during long winter days—the big, round, meaty tomatoes that are phenomenal not only as sandwich toppers but eaten on their own with a sprinkling of salt and a splash of balsamic vinegar. Favorites include 'Pink Berkeley Tie-Dye', 'Brandywine', 'Black Krim', 'Cherokee Purple', 'Costoluto Fiorentino', and 'Cosmonaut Volkov'.

PASTE TOMATOES. I tend to grow mostly these, because their thick, meaty flesh has a low water content that makes them ideal for sauces and canning. Many of these varieties tend to be determinate, which means that all the fruits ripen at the same time, allowing you to plan for processing big harvests. Favorites include 'Roma', 'Blue Beech', 'Heinz', and 'Amish Paste'.

Tips + Tricks

◆ Companion plant with basil, borage, chives, garlic, mint, nasturtium, and parsley. Keep tomato plants away from brassicas (cabbage, broccoli, cauliflower, and their relatives), corn, dill, and potatoes.

◆ Once tomato seeds have germinated, move the seedlings to grow under lights in a room with a temperature of 70°F/21°C. Keep the seedlings under the lights for 14 hours a day. (If you have windows that get great full-sun exposure, you can keep your seedlings on the sill.)

◆ Pot up into 3-inch pots when the seedlings develop their first set of true leaves.

◆ Harden off your tomato seedlings prior to transplanting. Start by placing the seedlings in a well-protected spot and slowly expose the seedlings to direct outside sunlight for a few hours each day. Over the course of a week or two, increase the amount of time outside.

◆ Take a clue from nature as to when it's ready for your tomatoes to go into the garden. Transplant tomatoes when bearded irises, flowering dogwood, and peonies are in full bloom. This is when evening temperatures regularly stay above 50°F/10°C—often 2 to 3 weeks after the last frost date.

◆ Avoid starting tomato seedlings too early. Smaller seedlings started closer to planting time experience less transplant shock, so they can focus on growing, whereas larger ones started earlier need more time to settle in.

◆ Transplant tomato plants deeply in the soil. This is good news for anyone with leggy seedlings! All those tiny hairs that grow along a tomato's stem become roots once underground.

◆ Dig a 12-inch-deep hole for each seedling. In the bottom of the hole, toss a handful or two of well-aged compost, plus a sprinkling of bonemeal. Both help promote healthy plants and early fruit ripening.

◆ Provide good, consistent watering for these tasty veggies, which are 95 percent water. Give each plant a good 1 to 2 inches of water a week by watering at the base. Avoid wetting the leaves to help prevent fungal and bacterial disease.

◆ Remove all foliage along the stem below the lowest cluster of ripening fruits. Tomatoes don't need a ton of foliage to produce a great crop. Removing excess leaves not only improves airflow and allows the sun's rays direct access to the fruit, it also helps mitigate potential diseases like blight and mildew.

Did you know that cooked tomatoes can be better for you than raw? The fruit's vitamin C content does take a hit, but nutrients like lycopene increase as heat breaks down the tomato's walls, helping our bodies absorb this beneficial antioxidant.

Determinate or Indeterminate?

Also known as bush tomatoes, determinate varieties grow to a certain height and are shorter and bushier. Their fruits ripen together at a similar time, making determinates a great choice for folks who want to process their harvests in big batches. Because of their limited growth, determinate tomatoes tend not to need pruning.

Indeterminate tomatoes grow vines and flowers all season long, until frost. They produce fruit until frost, too. Because these tomatoes grow and grow, they must be trellised to make them manageable and to help ward off disease. Indeterminate varieties create a lot of foliage, so it's smart to keep the suckers (those shoots that appear where the branch meets the stem) pruned to allow for better air circulation.

MAGIC GARDEN SPRAY

This magic spray saves plants—and sanity. Not only did this spray rescue my tomatoes several times from early blight, it also saved countless summer squash from powdery mildew madness. The best part is that you already have all the necessary ingredients right in your kitchen.

- 1 gallon water
- 3 tablespoons baking soda
- 1 tablespoon vegetable oil
- 1–2 drops dish soap

Combine the ingredients in a 1-gallon container, then pour the mixture into a 16-ounce refillable spray bottle. Spray thoroughly on plants, making sure to coat both sides of the leaves. Apply in the early morning or evening. Do not spray when the sun is high or during the hottest part of the day or you risk burning the foliage.

Why it works: Baking soda acts as a fungicide. Once applied, it changes the pH balance on the leaves and creates an environment in which the fungus that causes blight and mildew can no longer colonize.

Storing and Ripening Tomatoes

When it comes to storing fresh tomatoes, your fridge is their foe. Please promise me you'll never store your precious tomatoes in the fridge! It's just cruel, robbing both the tomato and you of its delicious flavor, which declines at temperatures under 55°F/13°C.

Ripen green tomatoes by placing them in a large brown paper bag and storing it in a cool, dark spot. Check them every few days and take out any ripened fruit. The only hard part is remembering that you have a bag of tomatoes stored away. That's not something you want to remember in February. Trust me.

If frost is coming, harvest any tomatoes with a hint of a blush and set these out in a warm room on a table or windowsill, where they'll ripen.

Preserving Tomatoes without Canning

I have three favorite ways to preserve tomatoes.

◆ The first is to slow roast and then freeze them packed in olive oil for midwinter happiness. Preheat the oven to 250°F/120°C. Start by cutting the tomatoes in half and placing them cut side up on a baking sheet. Drizzle with olive oil and sprinkle with minced thyme, oregano, and basil. Season with a dash of salt and some freshly ground black pepper. Roast for about 3 hours, until the tomatoes are soft and shriveled. Once cooled, store in an airtight container in the freezer, where they keep for 3 months. I love tossing these into chilis, sauces, and pizzas.

◆ The second method is to simmer them, strain out the seeds and skin, jar up the pulp, and freeze.

◆ The third way is my favorite lazy gardener's approach to saving the big, fat tomatoes of summer: Simply wash, dry, and core them. Space them apart on a baking sheet and freeze. Once frozen, store the tomatoes in freezer bags. Freezing on a baking sheet before packaging enables you to grab individual tomatoes, as opposed to an iceberg-size chunk, from the freezer.

EAT

THICK, RICH, ROASTED TOMATO SAUCE

I grew up helping my mom make vats of sauce on the weekends, as we transformed the kitchen into a mess of pots, sieves, skins, and seeds. When I first started making my own sauce, I followed my mom's instructions: Use only paste tomatoes, parboil to remove their skins, sieve with a food mill to remove the seeds, get them into the pot for cooking, then watch that pot simmer for hours on end to thicken the sauce. It only took me a few times of going through this process as an adult to realize that it's more work than it needs to be. Now I go from harvest to dinner plate in an hour, my sauce has never tasted better, and watery sauces are a thing of the past.

5 pounds tomatoes (paste tomatoes work great, but I mix together whatever varieties are ripe and ready: heirlooms, grape, paste, and even cherry tomatoes)
Olive oil
2 garlic cloves, minced
Thyme sprig, minced
Oregano sprig, chopped
A splash of wine (optional)
Basil sprig, chopped
Salt and freshly ground black pepper

1 Preheat the oven to 400°F/200°C. Line a baking sheet with parchment paper.

2 Cut the tomatoes in half and place cut side down on the baking sheet. Bake for 15 to 20 minutes. Drain the excess water from the tray, then remove the skin from the tomatoes. (I use tongs for this.) Place the tomatoes in a bowl and puree with a handheld blender. For a chunkier sauce, crush the tomatoes with a potato masher.

3 Pour a good drizzle of oil into a saucepan over medium heat and sauté the garlic for 30 seconds. Add the tomatoes, thyme, oregano, and wine (if using). Reduce the heat and simmer for 20 to 30 minutes. Remove from the heat and add the basil. Season to taste with salt and pepper.

PEPPERS

Peppers are a joy to have in the garden, even though it took me years and years to convince these warm-weather sun lovers that they can indeed grow in my Maine woods. But the wide array of varieties to try, of both sweet and hot peppers, means there is always something new to explore.

WHEN TO SOW
Start indoors 8 to 10 weeks before
the last frost date.

SOIL
Compost-rich, well-drained soil

PREFERRED LIGHT
Full sun for 6 to 8 hours a day

Tips + Tricks

GROWING

- Cover the growing site with tarps or black plastic to warm the soil for a week before planting. This reduces transplant shock and helps plants establish quicker.

- Go easy on the fertilizer and compost; too much causes excessive leaf growth and less fruit development. Once the plant begins to produce blossoms, apply a granular 5-10-10 fertilizer around the base of the plant.

- Pot up for a plethora of peppers whether you're planting in a garden or growing on a balcony. These container-loving vegetables prefer to be grown in 3- to 5-gallon pots.

- Pot up your peppers once the seedlings develop their first true leaves. The key to proper potting is to use the right size container. So, for the first potting up, transplant into a 2-inch pot. After a few weeks, it'll be time to pot up into the next size, 4 inches. Grow the seedling in that container until it's time to transplant outside.

- Northern gardeners should look for short-season varieties with early maturity dates for the best luck getting fruits to ripen before frost hits. 'King of the North' and 'Early Jalapeño' are both great varieties for cold climates.

USING

- Preserve peppers the easy way, by freezing them. Wash and dry the peppers thoroughly, then freeze them whole on a baking sheet. Once frozen, bag and store in the freezer. Or prep the peppers in your preferred way—chop, dice, slice—then freeze. No blanching or other prefreezing prep is required.

Companion plant with carrots, onions, nasturtiums, geraniums, zinnias, and a variety of herbs, from basil to dill to oregano.

'EARLY JALAPEÑO'. This is perfect for short-season growers, as it's early to harvest. Typically used when green, but when allowed to ripen to red, they'll have a slight fruity flavor. My favorite pepper to grow, it reaches 3½ inches long. The amount of heat is variable.

SHISHITO. Pick these thin-walled, slightly sweet peppers when green. They're mild overall, though purportedly 1 in 10 is hot (I haven't stumbled across any yet). Prolific, branching plant with fruit 2 to 4 inches long.

PADRÓN. These Spanish heirlooms are a delicious treat that make terrific tapas. Like shishitos, most are not very hot at all, until you get the one that is. Try these 1½-inch fruits stuffed with cheese.

'FISH'. This medium-hot African American heirloom vegetable is one of the prettiest peppers I grow. It features variegated leaves with 3-inch white-streaked fruits that ripen to an orange-red. Could easily be grown as an ornamental plant.

THAI. Word is, the smaller the pepper, the hotter it is. And this one packs a whole lot of heat in a very tiny pop! Compact, mounded plants produce 1½-inch-long fruits. Harvest when red. Amazing in stir-fries.

SERRANO. My go-to for our favorite homemade hot sauce. The fruits are red or orange when ripe. High-yielding plants have 3-inch fruits that look like smaller, thin jalapeños.

Did you know that drying peppers not only intensifies the heat and flavor of the pepper but also increases its natural sugars? So if you like your hot sauces and fermentations extra zesty, choose dried over fresh. Best of all, if properly stored, dried peppers can keep your life hot and spicy for many years.

To lessen the heat level of hot peppers, remove the white membrane. Counteract the capsicum's heat by drinking milk.

SHISHITO PEPPERS

THAI PEPPERS

PADRÓN

'FISH' PEPPERS

Top Your Hot Peppers

Most of a pepper plant's growth hormones live in the very top portion of the plant. So when you pinch off that top, it signals the plant to focus its energy on branching out rather than growing taller. And a bushier plant is not only more productive but also sturdier.

The best time to top peppers is after the plant has had a chance to develop a few sets of leaves and a good root system, since the process does shock the plant a bit initially. Using a pair of clean scissors, snip off the very top growing tip. Once topped, the plant will need up to a week to rebound. After that, you'll see leaves sprouting from the stem's side nodes.

EARLY JALAPEÑO

AUTUMN

150

CAYENNE

EAT

PICKLED JALAPEÑOS

MAKES ABOUT A QUART

8	jalapeños, thinly sliced
2	cups water
1½	cups apple cider vinegar
2	medium carrots, thinly sliced
2	bay leaves
2	teaspoons coarse salt
1	teaspoon sugar
¼	teaspoon black peppercorns

1 Place the jalapeños in a medium bowl. Bring the water, vinegar, carrots, bay leaves, salt, sugar, and peppercorns to a boil in a medium saucepan over medium-high heat. Reduce the heat and simmer for 2 minutes.

2 Pour the mixture over the jalapeños and let cool until it reaches room temperature.

3 Store in an airtight container in the refrigerator for up to 3 weeks.

SPICY HOT LEMON SIPPER

MAKES A HALF-GALLON

2	quarts water
1	large piece fresh ginger, chopped
1	fresh chile, deseeded and chopped
	Juice of 4 large lemons
	Maple syrup

1 Bring the water to a boil in a saucepan. Reduce the heat, add the ginger, and simmer partially covered for 20 minutes.

2 Remove from the heat. Add the chile, stir, cover, and let sit overnight.

3 The next day, strain the mixture through a fine-mesh sieve into a pitcher. Stir in the lemon juice, then sweeten to taste with maple syrup. Stir and sip.

PAN-SEARED SHISHITOS

Pan-seared shishito peppers make a delicious snack to nosh on. Heat a cast-iron skillet (or other heavy-bottomed pan) over medium-high heat. Wash and dry the peppers, then toss them with a good drizzle of olive oil in a large bowl. When the pan is hot, toss in the peppers and cook, giving the pan a good shake every couple of minutes, until the peppers are charred and blistered, 5 or 6 minutes.

ONIONS & LEEKS

Growing your own onions and leeks opens up a whole new world of stinking good varieties to try! These versatile vegetables run the gamut from cut-and-come again scallions to cippolini's tasty, tiny flat discs to gorgeous baseball-size orbs brimming with a zesty bite. Including these kitchen staples in your garden will offer happiness to the dinner plate and to neighboring plants—both onions and leeks make great companion plants, because their strong scent helps ward off pests.

WHEN TO SOW
Start indoors 10 to 12 weeks before the last frost date; transplant to the garden 4 to 6 weeks before the last frost date.

SOIL Loose, compost-rich, well-drained soil kept evenly watered

PREFERRED LIGHT
Full sun

Favorite Varieties

STORAGE: 'Southport Red Globe', 'Patterson', 'Blush'

CIPPOLINI: 'Redwing', 'Pompeii', 'Gold Coin'

BUNCHING SCALLIONS: 'Red Long of Tropea', 'Warrior Bunching'

LEEKS: 'King Richard'

Day length matters when it comes to selecting the best variety of bulbing onions for your hardiness zone. Short-day varieties, which require 10 to 12 hours of light, are good for southern growers. Long-day varieties, which require 14 to 16 hours of light, are good for northern growers. Intermediate-day varieties are good for most growers, except those on the northern and southern extremes of the US.

Tips + Tricks

- Companion plant with carrots, radishes, and rosemary.

- Sow in clusters and transplant out as such. Gently harvest an onion from one cluster at a time, allowing the remaining onions in the cluster to continue growing.

- Purchase new seed stock annually; these seeds have a short shelf life of just 1 year.

- Trim onion seedlings when they reach 5 inches tall to encourage them to grow bigger, thicker, stronger necks; this helps keep them from flopping once transplanted. Use clean, sharp shears to cut seedlings back to 2 to 3 inches in height. Depending on how long until you transplant, you may need to give them another trim later on.

- Fertilize these heavy feeders throughout the beginning of the growing season but stop feeding once the plant starts to bulb.

- Keep beds well weeded, because onions don't like the growing competition.

- Stop watering bulbing onions when their tops flop, usually around midsummer. Onion bulbs no longer require water at this stage. Withholding water also helps prevent the bulb from rotting and leaves from yellowing, making them better candidates for long-term storage.

- Leave a few leeks in the ground and be wowed not only by the incredibly gorgeous blooms they send out in their second year but also by the wide array of beneficial insects that visit them.

The sweeter the onion, the shorter the storage time.

Favorite Autumn Herbs

Autumnal harvests of herbs fill the soul with both glee and reflection. Glee because the garden is still offering up these delicious herbal gifts, and reflection as you realize that the growing season is coming to a close. It just makes each leaf taste sweeter.

Coriander

❋ Coriander is simply the seed of the cilantro plant. But fear not, cilantro haters can be coriander lovers. Some folks have a genetic variation on their olfactoryreceptor genes that makes cilantro's leaves taste strongly of soap. But that taste applies only to the leaves, not the seeds.

❋ Plant this annual herb in well-drained soil. It grows best in sun but tolerates partial shade.

❋ It has a long taproot, so it's best not to plant it in containers, unless they are very deep.

❋ Sow once and it'll self-sow for decades.

❋ Toast the seeds before using in recipes to bring out the aromatics and oils.

Catnip

❋ This bushy perennial thrives in full sun but will tolerate part shade.

❋ If cut back after the first flush of blooms, it will produce a second flush of leaves in late summer.

❋ It's a prolific self-seeder.

❋ Plan to harvest at once after the dew dries on a sunny day, right before the flowers fully open, when the plant's volatile oils are at their peak. Cut the entire plant back to 3 inches from the soil surface.

❋ To dry, hang in loose bunches in a cool, dry spot out of direct sunlight.

Not just a treat for kitties, catnip makes a delicious, calming cup of tea. To make this tea even tastier, steep with a few thin slices of apple or blend with chamomile.

Use the leaves as a poultice to soothe sunburns and skin irritations. Catnip even makes a good mosquito repellant.

Nasturtium

These South American beauties are fans of full sun, warmer weather, and warm, well-drained soil. Sow directly into the garden around the same time you transplant tomatoes and basil.

Some varieties create big, bushy displays perfect for border plantings, while others offer a trailing habit that will need support if you'd like it to climb a trellis. For smaller spaces, containers, and windowsills, look for compact varieties.

Nasturtium is considered an herb because of its culinary offerings. You can nosh on the leaves, and the seeds can be pickled and turned into garden capers. Its colorful flowers are edible as well. Stuff the flowers with an herb cheese, as you would with squash blossoms, for colorful treats to make a tasty memory.

Anise Hyssop

This is a short-lived perennial but an active self-seeder; if left to its own devices, you'll have an endless supply of anise hyssop for years to come.

They truly are the bee's knees of the garden. Long-lasting flowers bring in bees by the dozens, as well as many other beneficial pollinators.

The leaves offer a licorice scent and bite. Dried, they are great in teas and potpourris.

Don't cut back the seed heads in autumn: The seeds offer a nutritious buffet for birds, especially goldfinches.

CALENDULA

Calendula is your gateway herb to the medicinal realm. It is incredibly versatile both in the garden and out. Calendula is the perfect plant for anyone interested in taking their herbal and garden learnings up a notch.

WHEN TO SOW
Sow seeds indoors 4 to 6 weeks before your last frost date.

SOIL Well-drained soil

PREFERRED LIGHT
Full sun; tolerates part shade

Tips + Tricks

GROWING

- Choose this champion of companion planting to deter many garden pests, including cabbageworms when interplanted with brassicas. Plant with tomatoes, asparagus, peas, carrots, brassicas, and beans. Their roots even work with beneficial soil fungus to suppress nematodes.

- Provide this easy-to-grow herb with rich soil and full sun.

- Pluck those flowers to keep blooms going all the way to frost. The more flowers you pick, the more the plant will produce.

- Collecting calendula's seed is easy, but its seed viability declines rapidly. For the best germination rates, don't use seed more than 2 years old.

- Save yourself time and space by direct sowing rather than starting seed indoors. This fast grower shoots up quickly from seed in no time.

EATING

- Known as "poor man's saffron," calendula flowers can be used in butters, sauces, soups, and baked goods. The petals can also serve as a yellow food coloring.

Medicinal Properties

Anti-inflammatory, antibacterial, antifungal, antiviral, antispasmodic

'PACIFIC BEAUTY'

Favorite Varieties

'Resina' and 'Alpha' are my favorite varieties to grow, as they have the highest resin content, making them perfect for herbal concoctions. I also love 'Pacific Beauty' for its bright citrus shades and warm brown center, and 'Flashback' for its autumnal hues of apricot and gold with an underside of beautiful burgundy.

'ALPHA'

Tips for Drying & Using Calendula

- To dry, place the flower heads facedown on a wire rack or newspapers, making sure the flowers don't touch. Calendula petals are hygroscopic, which means they can absorb moisture from the air. Spacing flower heads so the petals do not overlap helps them dry better, which locks in their bold color.

- Because the petals are hygroscopic, be sure to store dried blossoms in a moisture-proof container.

- Use dried calendula, not fresh petals, in your infusions. Fresh flowers can cause bacteria to build up in the oil, rendering the oil rancid. Or allow fresh flowers to wilt for 24 hours before using so that moisture evaporates.

- When flowers are dry, jar them up for use later in skin-care treatments like infused oils, baths, and salves, or in the kitchen as a tea or a saffron substitute.

CALENDULA-INFUSED OIL

Herb-infused oils are a treasure for your skin and are so easy to make. Feel free to swap the calendula for another herb of your choice, or create a mix of herbs.

Fill a clean mason jar two-thirds full with dried calendula flowers. Pour oil to within an inch of the top of the jar. (I use olive oil for winter months and a lighter apricot oil for summertime.) Using a wooden spoon, slowly and gently muddle the herbs in the oil. Use a clean bamboo skewer to skim along the inside edge of the jar to make sure all air pockets are popped. Seal with a cap and keep in a cool, dark cabinet. Give the jar a gentle shake every few days. In 6 weeks, your infused oil will be ready to be strained and jarred for using.

CALENDULA SALVE

Calendula is a miracle worker for your skin. It promotes both the growth and healing of tissue. We use this balm for everything from softening rough gardeners' hands to soothing eczema to even rubbing on our pup Cobbs's paws when they get chapped.

Place 3½ ounces calendula-infused oil and ½ ounce beeswax in a double boiler. Heat over low to medium heat until the wax is melted. Remove from the heat and pour quickly into tins or jars (move swiftly; this salve hardens fast). This amount will fill two 2-ounce tins.

OREGANO

Consider this my ode to oregano! This is the plant that inspired me to stop separating my herbs and start interplanting them with vegetables and flowers. Of course, oregano is brimming with amazing culinary and medicinal uses, but this aromatic herb also makes for a stunning plant out in the garden. Plant a few seedlings along a front border, and within just a few weeks it'll become a lush, bushy mini hedgerow that looks impressive with very little effort. That's my kind of plant.

WHEN TO SOW
Start seeds indoors 6 to 8 weeks before the last frost date.

SOIL Well-drained soil

PREFERRED LIGHT
Full to part sun

Medicinal Properties
Chock-full of flavonoids (which ward off toxins), carvacrol (antimicrobial and antioxidant agent), and rosmarinic acid (prevents cell damage); a powerful antibiotic

Tips + Tricks

GROWING

◆ Companion plant with the vegetable of your choice, as oregano's chemical compounds repel insects.

◆ Promote bushy, big plants by pinching back the herb throughout the season.

◆ Propagate by division in spring, dividing clumps every 3 years. You can also propagate via stem cuttings.

◆ Trim the entire plant once a month to control its encroachment on neighboring plants.

◆ Avoid overwatering this arid-loving herb. Oregano doesn't like to sit in water, so strive to water only when the soil is dry to the touch.

◆ Provide extra air circulation to keep root rot at bay when growing oregano in humid areas.

◆ Plant Greek oregano for the best-tasting leaves.

◆ Increase the pollination rates of neighboring vegetables with this pollinator favorite. Bees go all abuzz over oregano's flowers and will certainly boost the development of fruiting vegetables.

EATING

◆ Incorporate oregano's edible flowers into salads and side dishes.

Ways to Preserve the Harvest

Frozen flavor pods. One of my favorite ways to put herb trimmings to good use is to make frozen flavor pods with them. Wash and dry your oregano, chop it finely, and put it into ice cube trays. Cover with a good-quality olive oil and freeze. Once frozen, pop out and store the cubes in an airtight freezer bag. Whenever you need to add an herbal punch to a dish, just grab a pod and toss it in. Flavor pods are great for marinades, sautés, sauces, pasta—anything! Play around with different herbal blends for your flavor pods.

Dries like a dream. Oregano is an ideal herb to dry, as its flavor improves when moisture evaporates. Hang to dry in small bunches of 6- to 8-inch stems. The benefit of hanging is that all those important essential oils drop down to the leaves, sealing in the best taste, smell, and nutritional benefits. Store the dried bunches in a glass jar. When you need some dried herb, just give a bunch a gentle squeeze to release some leaves, then put the bunch back in the jar.

Pet protection. Help repel insects and ticks from your fur friends with this oregano infusion. Grab a medium heatproof bowl, then pour 2 cups boiling water over 2 tablespoons dried oregano. Let it steep until the water cools to room temperature. Strain and pour into a spray bottle. Spray as needed, but avoid spraying around your pet's eyes.

How to Dry & Store Herbs

I prefer to air-dry my herbs, since exposing them to any type of heat zaps away some of their essential oil. Depending on the herb, I dry on screens, on racks, in baskets, or by hanging in bunches.

* Dry herbs in a humidity-free, well-ventilated room out of direct sun.

* If using a screen or rack, arrange herbs in a single layer for good air circulation; this also helps retain the herb's color.

* Hang herbs like sage, lavender, catnip, oregano, and mint in loose, small bunches. (A benefit of hanging in bunches is that the herb's essential oils flow down into the drying leaves.)

* When hanging herbs in bunches, avoid tying them tightly together; that could trap moisture and invite mold.

* Thicker-stemmed herbs are best dried flat.

* If you plan to store your herbs as hanging bunches, cover each bunch with a paper bag (punching a few air holes in the bag first) to protect it from dust.

* Check on your drying herbs every few days. For herbs drying on screens or in baskets, give them a good shake, toss, and inspection.

* When the herbs are easily crumbled (signaling they are completely dry), store them in glass mason jars.

OTHER TIPS FOR DRYING HERBS

If you live in a high-humidity area or don't have space to dry your herbs here, there, and everywhere, here are two other options.

Drying in a dehydrator. Set the dehydrator for a temperature between 95 and 110°F/35 and 43°C. Make sure you've blotted off any dew or moisture, then spread them out in a single layer on the racks. Some herbs dry in an hour; others take much longer. Just keep an eye on them. Once the herbs crumble to the touch, jar them up.

Drying in an oven. Set your oven to the lowest temperature possible, ideally around 100°F/38°C, although that's hard to achieve with today's ovens. The herbs will need some air circulation while in the oven, so prop open the oven door slightly with something nonflammable. Keep a close eye on your herbs and pull them out when they crumble between your fingers.

Storage. Store dried herbs in glass containers, checking them every week or so for the first few weeks to make sure all is well and there's no hint of mildew in the jars. Put those precious jars in a cool spot out of direct light. Kept well, those herbs will easily last 6 months, with many keeping their flavor well up to 1 year. Over time, the herb's flavor and scent will begin to fade. That's when it's time to jar up a new batch.

Use the stems! By the way, after stripping the tasty leaves from rosemary, oregano, mint, basil, and sage, don't toss those stems. Rather, let them dry, then tie into bundles and use as aromatic fire starters for your woodstove, campfire, or fireplace.

Combining herbs with salt is probably my favorite way to preserve my garden's herbal happiness.

EAT

ROSEMARY-LEMON SALT

Once you make your own herbal salt, you'll never use regular salt again. This rosemary-lemon partnership is certain to please any dish it's used on.

MAKES 14 OUNCES

- 1½ ounces fresh rosemary leaves
- ½ ounce lemon peel
- 1¾ cups coarse sea salt
- 1 cup kosher salt
- ¼ cup fine sea salt

Place the rosemary, lemon, and ½ cup of the coarse sea salt in a food processor. Pulse several times to chop the herbs. Continue to add ½ cup of the salts at a time, pulsing after each addition until well combined.

Preheat the oven to 200°F/95°C. Spread the herb-salt mixture in a thin layer on a baking sheet. Bake for 1 hour, stirring and respreading the mixture with a spatula every 15 minutes, or until the rosemary leaves and salt are completely dry and crumbly. Let cool on the baking sheet. Once completely cooled, package in glass jars.

Favorite Autumn Flowers

A huge smile spreads across my face when I think of how grateful I am for these autumn bloomers. Come autumn, the days begin to cool and shorten. Because my garden is nestled in the woods, I feel the coolness and diminished sunlight even more sharply. The flowers that command my garden at this time of year are true powerhouses; they prevail with a proliferation of petals all the way to frost. When everything else starts to wither and fade, these flowers still shine bright, giving the soul one more good dose of fuel to keep garden dreams rolling throughout the snowy days ahead.

Sunflowers

❋ Companion plant with corn, squash, and pole beans. This "four sisters" method also maximizes growing space.

❋ Direct sow, if possible. Sunflower's delicate roots detest disturbance. If starting indoors and transplanting, sow the seed 4 weeks before the last frost date in a container that can be directly planted into the ground.

❋ Sow seed or transplant at the same time you transplant your tomatoes, peppers, and basil. Sunflowers prefer warm soil. Water deeply once a week.

❋ Succession sow every 3 weeks until the end of June for endless blooms until frost.

❋ Plant sunflowers in a row, then grow morning glories, runner beans, and squash with them to make a living wall of green gorgeousness.

❋ Bee kind to your pollinator pals and avoid planting pollen-free hybrids in favor of nectar-rich open-pollinated/heirloom varieties.

❋ Leave the seed heads for a fall feast for your local wildlife. Don't cut back the stalks come fall. Leave them as both a valuable food source and a shelter for insects (many slumber away the winter inside the protection of the thick stalk).

❋ Although flower heads follow the sun when they're young, once they fully mature, they stay facing east.

Echinacea

🌼 Echinacea loves average soil in full sun but isn't afraid of some light shade.

🌼 Sow seeds indoors 8 to 10 weeks before the last frost date.

🌼 Unlike other perennials, division is not recommended; propagate from seed or root cuttings.

🌼 It blooms summer through fall and is deer resistant and drought tolerant.

🌼 Plant en masse for a stunning visual impact.

🌼 Pollinators of all sorts will flock to echinacea's striking blooms. It's especially attractive to native bees.

🌼 Pair with rudbeckia, bee balm, and phlox for pure beauty.

🌼 Leave the seed heads come autumn, as they provide a nutrient-rich food source for your hungry bird friends. The birds will return your kindness by sprinkling some seeds so that volunteer plants pop up next spring.

🌼 Not all species of the *Echinacea* genus are equally medicinal; the more cultivated varieties don't offer the same herbal benefits. If growing for medicinal use, sow *E. purpurea* or *E. angustifolia*. Because of its popularity, wild echinacea has been overforaged, putting this plant at risk, so it's best to grow your own.

Larkspur

🌼 Larkspur likes full sun but will tolerate part shade. It thrives in compost-rich, well-drained soil.

🌼 This is an active self-sower. I struggled for years with my own larkspur seedlings that failed to flourish in the garden. It wasn't until the larkspur grew themselves from volunteers that I saw what strapping, bountiful plants they could be. They have become one of the most rewarding blooms I grow, and the best part is, they literally grow themselves.

🌼 The seeds need exposure to cold to germinate. It's best to direct seed in early spring or chill the seed in the refrigerator for 5 days before sowing indoors 6 to 8 weeks before the last frost date.

🌼 Deadhead the first blooms when finished for a second flush of flowers.

🌼 Looks best when planted in large groupings.

🌼 Makes a beautiful dried flower that keeps its hue for years.

Rudbeckia

❋ Start seed indoors 6 to 8 weeks before the last frost date.

❋ Light is needed for germination, so do not cover the seed after sowing. Rather, gently pat the seed onto the top of the soil to help anchor it once watered.

❋ Plant once and you'll have rudbeckia for life: It's an active self-seeding perennial.

❋ Prefers full sun and well-drained soil.

❋ Deadhead throughout the early summer to encourage more blooms.

❋ Divide the clumps every 4 years.

❋ Come late summer, leave the seed heads, as they provide a valuable food source for birds through autumn and winter.

Nicotiana

❋ Enjoys full sun but tolerates part shade. Likes well-drained, moist soil.

❋ Active self-sower in the garden.

❋ Start seeds indoors 4 to 6 weeks before the last frost date.

❋ Pinch back seedlings to encourage branching and bushiness.

❋ Seeds need light for germination.

❋ Taller varieties make good back-of-the-garden plants.

❋ Acts as a "trap crop" for tomato hornworms—the worms are drawn to the nicotiana instead of the tomatoes.

❋ Attracts hummingbirds and butterflies.

Zinnias

❋ These prolific blooms offer non-stop color all season long. The more you pick, the more flowers will grow.

❋ Easy to grow and low maintenance, sun-loving zinnias are drought tolerant, don't need fertilizer, and will grow in any type of soil.

❋ A few must-grow varieties: 'Queeny Lime Orange', 'Northern Lights Blend', 'Cactus Flowered Mix', 'Cut and Come Again', 'Peppermint Stick', and 'Thumbelina'.

❋ Seeds are easy to save: Just wait until they have completely dried on the plant before collecting.

❋ Your pollinator pals prefer single-headed varieties like 'Cut and Come Again' over showier double blooms like the 'Cactus Flowered' variety. To score extra pollinator points, plant pink and red varieties.

❋ Zinnias are often susceptible to powdery mildew. Help keep that at bay by watering at the base of the plant.

HOW TO DRY FLOWERS

Harvest in the morning as soon as the dew dries but before the flowers are wide open. (Fully ripe flowers drop their petals once dried.) Strip the leaves off each stem. Hang in loose bunches in an area out of direct sun and humidity but with good air circulation.

Everlasting Flower Love

I started growing everlasting flowers a few years back, and with the opening of my very first strawflower bloom, I was hooked. That led to expanding my collection to include statice, yarrow, celosia, gomphrena, and many, many more. Then I discovered that less-obvious everlastings—like larkspur, salvia, and chive and leek blossoms—make the most fetching keepers, too, holding on to their color beautifully.

Each week, another gaggle of bouquets gets hung from my studio rafters. Come the end of the season, just as the first nips of frost nibble and the garden begins to go to sleep, I no longer have to say a sad goodbye. Rather, I simply gaze up at the flower- and herb-filled rafters, and instantly, I'm back in the garden. My original intent in first growing these gorgeous flowers was to use them in projects and crafts. Turns out, my favorite way to use them is to just have them hang out in my studio with me as eye candy for the soul.

BUNNY TAILS

CELOSIA

LOVE-IN-A-MIST
AND HYDRANGEA

Best Flowers to
GROW FOR
DRYING

Bunny tails

Celosia

Chives

Echinacea

Goldenrod

Gomphrena

Hydrangea

Larkspur

Lavender

Leek flowers

Love-in-a-mist
(flowers and pods)

Poppy pods

Queen Anne's lace

Roses

Rudbeckia

Salvia

Statice

Strawflowers

Sweet Annie

Violas

Yarrow

GOMPHRENA

STRAWFLOWERS

YARROW

169

A Botanical Wreath

There's no wrong way to make these wreaths. I prefer to make simple, quick ones, but I'm completely enamored of the wreaths of art I see some folks achieve.

First, forage for twigs or vines to create the wreath's form. Use fresh twigs that are narrow and have a bit of bend to them. Twist the twigs or vines into a circle, and tie together in a few spots using twine or wire.

Form flowers into mini bundles and attach to the wreath. With some wreaths, you can simply weave the bundle into the form and it'll stay. With other forms, the flowers may need assistance to stay put; if so, use wire or jute to attach the bundles to the form. Add filler, as desired. I love saving seedpods and bunny tails to insert as fun fillers.

Decide how you'd like to hang the wreath. That can be an art unto itself! You can hang it on a nail or hook on the wall, or hang it from a ribbon sash. String together several wreaths to make a gorgeous garland.

How to Collect & Store Seed

If you're new to saving seeds, start with bean and pea seeds. They're easy to dry, fun to shell, gorgeous to behold, and simple to store. If you do plan on saving seed to replant, grow heirloom (open-pollinated) varieties instead of hybrids (which do not produce seeds that grow like the parent plant). Save seed from the healthiest, strongest plants.

As you continue to streamline your seed saving over the years, you can save your favorite heirloom seed *and* select for specific traits you like. For example, you can select for tomatoes that ripen early by specifically saving the seed from that heirloom plant's first fruit. Or if you want humongous zinnias, save only the seed from the biggest blooms. Plant that seed the next year, then once again save only seed from the biggest blooms. Do this a few more times and eventually your saved seeds will produce only big, beautiful blooms. And by cultivating your heirloom seeds over the years, you'll eventually grow strains of plants specifically bred to thrive in your very garden.

TIPS FOR SEED-STORAGE SUCCESS

Keep seeds in a cool spot with a consistent temperature, no moisture, and out of direct sunlight. Your best storage bet is to put your seeds in a sealed glass container (it must be moisture-proof) and store in your freezer or refrigerator.

If you are storing seeds in a sealed container, it is extremely important that the seeds be 100 percent dry or mold will develop. You can add some rice to the container to wick away any possible moisture.

These storage guidelines aren't just for loose seeds; they're also for your seed packets. I've been guilty of forgetting a packet or two of seeds in the greenhouse or, sometimes, right out on a garden bed. I learned the hard way that by doing that, I damaged the likelihood of the seeds' germinating due to their exposure to high temperatures, sun, and humidity.

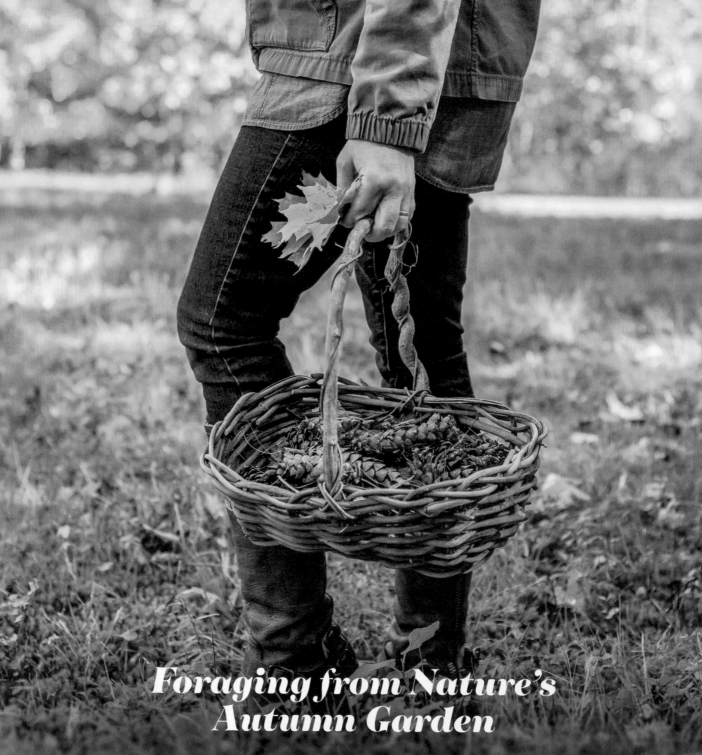

Foraging from Nature's Autumn Garden

Foraging in autumn feels akin to a squirrel collecting nuts for winter. Autumn is less obvious about its foraging treasures, yet there's something so reflective about gathering them. Perhaps that's because you need to stroll a little slower to see the trinkets. That gives you time both to reflect on the closing of the sea- days ahead. Or it could just be that the crisp autumn air seems to make everything feel a bit more exhilarating. Whatever it is, heading out to the woods, basket in hand, and returning with a collection of pinecones, bark, acorns, and more, makes you feel like you're bringing home a basket of gold.

Collecting &
Preserving
Pinecones and Acorns

Turns out, squirrels aren't the only ones around here gathering acorns for winter. In fall, baskets, bowls, and trays of pinecones and acorns completely cover our dining room table, thanks to a habit I've developed of bringing as much nature indoors as possible as winter approaches. I used to brag that I don't have a lot of trinkets in my house, but the truth is, I'm probably just a step away from being a woodland hoarder.

THE SUMMER OF ACORNS AND CHIPMUNKS

Living in the woods naturally entails living with chipmunks. If, like me, you're an active feeder of birds, that'll come with even more chipmunks. And if you have lots of oak trees around, you'll have lots more critters. After over a decade of observing our local wildlife, I've learned about acorn mast years and their rippling effect on wildlife.

During a mast year, oaks shed their acorns in bumper crops. They drop acorns everywhere—everywhere! These mast sheds happen about 2 out of every 10 autumns.

The summer following a mast year may as well be deemed the Summer of Chipmunks. That acorn jackpot leads to a greater birth rate of all sorts of woodland critters. It's normal to have squirrels and chipmunks in the garden, but much like those mast-year acorns, these critters will be *everywhere*! Your garden is their mecca.

But fear not, the next summer will be better. Why? Well, autumn rolls around again and because there's an all-you-can-eat buffet of chipmunks, guess who's coming to dinner? Owls! And because there's so much for them to feast on, the owl birth rate shoots up, so you'll see more and more owls and fewer and fewer chipmunks.

Acorn Ornaments

Channel your inner squirrel and start gathering acorns to make a few charming ornaments or strings of fetching garlands. The secret to success is using eyelet screws: tiny circles with a tiny screw base that you can carefully screw into the top of your acorn and/or pinecone to make for easy hanging or stringing.

Start by preserving the acorns so that you can keep these decorations for years to come. Select acorns with no holes in them. Remove the brown cap from the acorn body and set it aside. Soak the acorns in a bowl of water for 20 minutes. Give them a good swirl and scrub to remove any dirt. Strain and lay the acorns across a tea towel on a rack and let dry for 1 hour. Then spread the acorns in a single layer on a baking sheet and bake in a 200°F/95°C oven for 1 to 2 hours. Keep the oven door slightly ajar during baking to allow the acorns' moisture to escape.

Now that your acorns are preserved, it's time to paint them if you please. You can also apply a clear varnish if desired. Or do as I do and just let them be their glorious selves.

The next step is to reunite the acorn bodies with their little brown caps. It doesn't matter if a cap is not a perfect fit: Use a glue gun to dab a small blob of glue to the inside of the cap and press it onto the body of the acorn to seal the deal.

Use an awl and make a small divot in the top of the cap. Take an eyelet screw, place in the divot, and gently screw into the cap. Now you're ready to hang your ornaments or string your garland!

PINECONE BIRD FEEDER

Come mid-November, as whispers of winter's imminent arrival become louder and louder, birds become hungrier for seed, looking for food to keep them fed and warm. Making these fun feeders to offer as early holiday treats not only provides important sustenance to our feathered friends but may also become a beloved family tradition.

The first step is to preserve the pinecones (this also allows you to save them for other crafts). Preheat the oven to 200°F/95°C and line a baking sheet with aluminum foil. Place the pinecones on the sheet and bake for 30 minutes, or until the resin becomes clear. *Note: Pinecones can be flammable, so don't leave the oven unattended.*

Once baked and cooled, tie a string to the top of a pinecone for hanging. Using a spatula, coat the cone in peanut butter or suet. Place birdseed in a mixing bowl and roll the coated pinecone in the seed, mashing the seed gently into the pinecone's crevices. Hang outside in a spot where you'll be able to gaze at it.

Road-Tripping for Winterberries

Every year after the Thanksgiving holiday, we pile into the car and go a-hunting for sprigs of beautiful winterberries. These striking native bushes grow in swampy roadside areas and display their red berries after they shed their leaves, adding a little holiday magic to the landscape. The berries provide a critical food source for birds during autumn and winter; the branches we bring home will go on our deck, in hopes of attracting the likes of chickadees, cardinals, and cedar waxwings.

BERRIED BUSHES FOR BIRDS

Here are a few great shrubs that your wildlife friends will flock to each winter: American Washington hawthorn, black chokecherry, northern bayberry, staghorn sumac, viburnums, and winterberry holly.

Winter

A Time to Rest

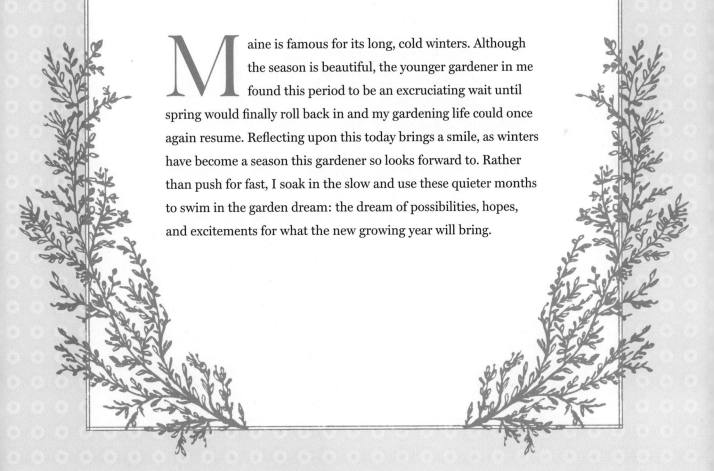

Maine is famous for its long, cold winters. Although the season is beautiful, the younger gardener in me found this period to be an excruciating wait until spring would finally roll back in and my gardening life could once again resume. Reflecting upon this today brings a smile, as winters have become a season this gardener so looks forward to. Rather than push for fast, I soak in the slow and use these quieter months to swim in the garden dream: the dream of possibilities, hopes, and excitements for what the new growing year will bring.

Bring houseplants back indoors before first frost. Water less and avoid fertilizing in winter, as most plants are in their dormant period.

Overwintering Indoors

Each winter, my studio is filled with pots of geraniums, begonias, and stem cuttings of everything from coleus and cup-and-saucer vines to several different herbs, including rosemary and lavender. Over the holidays, I add in a few pots of poinsettias, and come February, I always stock up on a few pots of roses from our local supermarket.

Being surrounded by dozens of plants of all sorts warms up winter. It can keep you connected to something green, which is often what the garden soul craves the most. It's also soothing to have these plants to tend to as your garden hibernates (though truth be told, most houseplants are also dormant during winter, so the tending is kept to a minimum).

Groundhog Day marks the halfway point between winter and spring. As winter wanes, it's time to repot your houseplants, give the overwintered pots of garden plants on your windowsill a light feeding, and pot up those stem cuttings. Once your weather becomes consistently warm, slowly harden off the plants you'd like to bring out to the garden, along with the potted-up stem cuttings. Once acclimated, transplant your stem cuttings and place your pots of overwintered garden happiness wherever your heart guides.

Use the quieter months to dream of possibilities, hopes, and excitements for what the new growing year will bring.

 GROW

Geraniums for Year-Round Blooms

Geraniums are a favorite to overwinter indoors because they bloom all year long. Here's how to do it: Dig up the plant. Repot. I sometimes cut the plant back to 4 to 6 inches above the soil, which encourages it to grow bushier. But if I'd like to bask in the blooms, I tend not to cut it back, and it can become straggly. In that case, I usually cut the plant back a bit come late spring once it has transitioned outside.

If you choose to cut back your plant, try rooting those cuttings to make more plants. Let your cuttings sit out for 18 to 24 hours before putting them in water or rooting hormone.

Note: Geraniums are toxic to pets.

POINSETTIAS IN THE GARDEN

Poinsettias are fun plants to incorporate into your garden as container plants. Although known more as a plant for Christmas decor, poinsettias are actually a tropical perennial. After the holidays, rehome your poinsettia to a sunny spot in a room that stays between 60 and 70°F/16 and 21°C. The brightly colored leaves will fall, but fear not, there's plenty of life left in the plant. To encourage a bushier habit, trim your plant back after the leaves have dropped. Cut it to 4 inches above the soil. Feed. Come summer, move the plant outside to soak in the sun and warmth, but make sure temps are holding at or above 65°F/18°C before you put it out. At summer's end, it'll be time to bring the poinsettia back inside. Before you do, give it another trim, this time just slightly cutting back to once again encourage branching. Repot and feed.

The Best Time to Propagate Houseplants

With its increased day length, spring is the best time to propagate plants from cuttings. Houseplants will be waking up from dormancy and ready to grow, grow, grow, making them primed for propagation. Plus, after their long winter's nap, those houseplants could probably use a good haircut—a win-win for both the mother plant and your future happy plants from cuttings. Just be sure to sterilize those scissors before snipping to mitigate the transfer of any disease or bacteria. Also, give your freshly potted-up plants a good feeding of fertilizer to help them settle into their new homes.

Stem Cuttings: The Easy Way to Propagate

Rosemary is one of my favorite garden herbs, but it can be so frustrating to start from seed. Poor germination and snail-slow growth often make growing rosemary feel like more work than it's worth. Stem cuttings are the perfect way to make more rosemary plants; it gives you a huge leap ahead in terms of plant size and vigor. Plus, seeing those jars of cuttings all along your windowsill will make you happy.

Here are a few tips for successful stem cuttings.

✳ Any woody herb works great for this type of propagation—mint, sage, thyme, rosemary, lavender, and oregano. You can also root up other plants like coleus and ivy. Have fun and experiment trying to root different things.

✳ Take your cuttings from a healthy plant—either during spring, when houseplants and overwintered garden plants are coming out of dormancy, or during summer, when garden plants are growing vigorously. As a general rule, take cuttings from the parent plant's new growth. That said, sometimes I've had more rooting success with woodier herbs when I take a cutting that has a bit of both new and old growth to it.

✳ Keep your cuttings on the north side of your house, out of direct sun.

✳ Be patient: These things can take time. Some plants sprout roots in just a week; for others, it can be well over a month before any signs of life appear.

✳ If a cutting tries to develop flower buds (like my coleus babies like to do), nip that bud right off. The cutting needs to focus its energy on creating roots, not flowers.

✳ Don't get discouraged if you don't have immediate success. Results can be hit or miss, so go into the propagation process with a few more cuttings than you think you really need.

HOW TO

Take Stem Cuttings

1 Snip a 6-inch-long stem that has both a bit of new and old growth on it.

2 Gently strip off the lower 2 to 3 inches of leaves. Place the cutting in a small jar of water and keep on a windowsill.

3 Replace the water every 2 to 3 days, giving the jar a quick cleaning as well to remove any slime and soft or rotting stems. This is a key step!

4 In anywhere from 2 to 8 weeks, you should see happy little roots sprouting. Some plants—like mint, coleus, basil, and oregano—sprout quickly. Others—such as lavender and rosemary—could take well over a month.

5 Once a healthy root system has been established, pot the new plant in soil and give it good light.

6 After it has acclimated to pot life, pinch the tips of your cuttings to encourage branching out. Treat your plant to a very light feeding of fertilizer after pinching.

Are Fungus Gnats Lurking
in Your Potting Mix?

Every February, I take over our dining room to start seedlings. This seed-starting strategy worked great, until one year when I kept seeing gnats flying all around my seedlings. I couldn't figure out where the gnats were coming from, as there were no plants in the house. Soon after that, my seedlings began to lose their vigor. They weakened, and their growth stagnated. Upon closer inspection, I discovered maggots in the soil and quickly learned that I was dealing with fungus gnats. The worst part? I realized they had arrived in a bag of potting mix.

Fungus gnats are a pest that you need to attack in two different life stages, the adult flies and the larvae,

to get them successfully under control. The larvae feed on the delicate seedling root hairs that are critical to healthy plant development. They can also cause damping-off in seedlings. Damping-off not only hampers growth, it more often than not causes the seedling to die. It is caused by mold or fungus that thrives in chilly, wet soil.

All it takes is a tiny hole in a bag of potting mix, and a fungus gnat can fly in and make itself at home. Rich, organic soil is the most attractive to these pests. Because of this, it's good to get into the practice of sterilizing your soil before using it (see page 183).

Fungus Gnats from Your New Plant Friend

Another way fungus gnats can be brought unknowingly into your home is with the arrival of a new houseplant. It's easy to be so excited to welcome a new plant that you slip it right into your current jungle of houseplants, only to quickly realize that with your new plant came a hoard of unwanted guests that are now frolicking with wild abandon among the rest of your plants. Err on the side of caution and treat each new plant with a diluted hydrogen peroxide solution. Simply mix one part hydrogen peroxide with four parts water. Pour the solution at the plant's base until the soil is fully saturated and the solution runs out the bottom of the pot. This will eradicate any fungus gnat larvae in the soil.

Here are other tips to tackle fungus gnats.

✳ Use yellow sticky traps to nab the adult gnats, preventing them from laying eggs.

✳ Drench the soil with neem oil.

GROW

MANAGING MILDEW

Mildew can be common indoors, especially in winter, with its fluctuating temperatures and poor air circulation. Trim off the affected areas with a clean pair of scissors. Make a mixture of one part milk to four parts water and pour it into a spray bottle. Spray the plant and promptly place it under a bright lamp, in direct sun, or in a bright, sunny spot: Bright light activates milk's mildew-killing powers. After a few days, the white powdery coating should be gone and calm will be restored.

HOW TO

Sterilize Your Potting Mix

1 Fill a large pan or bowl with the new potting mix.

2 Bring a kettle of water to a boil.

3 Pour enough boiling water over the potting mix so that it is thoroughly moistened. Stir to ensure full saturation; add more water if needed.

4 Cover the pan with aluminum foil or plastic wrap and let the potting mix cool to room temperature.

5 Keep the mix covered until you're ready to use it.

Dream Green:
Soak In the Joy of Garden Planning

During the first 15 years of my gardening journey, the period between when one growing season ended and the next began would feel excruciatingly long. Maine winters are notoriously cold and seemingly endless, and my bleak outlook regarding how long it would be before I'd be back out in the garden would bring on a bit of fretting and impatience. Now I'm practically begging January to slow down a bit.

The reason is because I changed my outlook and approach to these barren, frigid months. Rather than drudging through winter, waiting until I could sow that first seed, I now celebrate the slowness of the season, diving deep into the dream of what the new growing season may bring. My favorite way to do this is in my garden planning. I toss aside the graph paper and any rigidity and instead grab paintbrushes, paper, and watercolors. With the first blob of color on the page, I begin to dream in possibilities, wishes, and hopes. Outside my window the world may be blanketed in snow, but here, on my dining room table, by the woodstove, I swim in vivid color, brightness, and a vibrancy that the soul needs this time of year.

Here are a few things to take into consideration when planning your garden.

Sunlight and shade. Which spots on your plot are sunny and for how long? Is the sun blocked at any point in the season? Because I have a woodland garden, I always have to be mindful that in spring my garden gets full sun, but once the trees' leaves unfurl, my garden is mainly in partial shade. Come early September, we have to wrestle with the fact that the sun doesn't rise above the tree line, so even though the temps are still good for growing, the garden is mainly in full shade.

Crop rotation. Growing the same crops in the same bed year after year can deplete the soil of the nutrients needed to grow those crops. Crop rotation helps keep soil's fertility healthy and reduces soilborne diseases and pests. Some crops—such as lettuce, cabbage, squash, tomatoes, and corn—are heavy feeders, depleting the soil of many valuable nutrients. To keep the soil healthy and balanced, follow heavy-feeding crops with ones that give back to the soil, like legumes. Or follow with light feeders like root vegetables and herbs.

The other key is to remember that crop rotation applies to entire vegetable families. That means it's not a good idea to follow broccoli with kale or cabbage, because they are all brassicas. The same goes for squash and cucumbers, or tomatoes and peppers.

Companion planting. This is my mantra for organic gardening. See more about this on page 76.

Succession planting. There are a couple of approaches to succession sowing. One is to sow initial seedings of quick-growing veggies like lettuce, radishes, and carrots in smaller sowings spaced every 2 to 3 weeks throughout the course of the summer (taking a break during the hottest periods of the growing season). By planting like this, you're guaranteed fresh nibbles of these vegetables all season long. Another way is to follow one quick-growing crop with another, like spring lettuce with summer squash, which I then follow with fall peas or a short-season bean. This approach lets me grow three different crops in the same space across the season.

Intercropping. This is when you plant short-season varieties in the same bed as longer-growing veggies, such as growing lettuce with your tomatoes. The lettuce will be ready for harvest long before the tomato plants overgrow them. Radishes and carrots are another great partnership; the radishes are ready for harvest long before the carrots take off. By growing these two together, the carrots benefit from the radishes' keeping the soil loose, allowing for better carrot germination and root development.

Plants' needs. Is it a short plant that's best grown in borders, or is it a tall planting of dill that begs to be in the background? Besides keeping in mind a plant's height, take note of its width as well; big, bushy plants like squash may need extra space.

Color and blossoms. If you want to get all fancy (especially you flower growers out there), toss color combinations and bloom times into the garden-planning mix. As you plan, dream up how the color flows through your garden—whether that's color of flowers or of veggies. One of my favorite views in my garden is a big bed of kale in all different textures and varied hues of green, purple, and red. Tuck a little companion planting of calendula into this colorful bed and you've just created a heavenly sight.

Reading this list might seem overwhelming, but trust me—if you sit down and plan little by little over several weeks, not only will your garden vision come together, but it'll seep into your subconscious. Come that first day of spring, when you sow with wild abandon, you'll probably be doing it in a more informed way than you give yourself credit for, because of all your research and learning leading up to that first seed going into the ground.

Seed-Starting Prep

You wouldn't immediately associate winter with the start of seed sowing, but considering that winter isn't ushered in until December 21 and doesn't give way to spring until March 20, those three cold months are prime seed-starting time. Think about when your first seed catalogs start to arrive: probably well before the holiday season gets into full gear, right? And if you're like me, rather than having visions of sugarplums dancing in your head, you're dreaming of seed packets of all the different veggies, herbs, and flowers you can't wait to grow. So help melt winter's chill by dreaming and having warm thoughts of all things green and gardeny.

Ordering Seeds

'Tis the season to gaze impatiently out the window toward the mailbox while waiting for the seed catalog parade to begin. It's one of my favorite times of year—so much so that I now plan a daylong event where I squirrel myself away with my stack of catalogs, a garden journal, a plethora of pens, and plenty of nibbles, and just dream green.

When selecting a seed company to order from, choose one that suits how you garden. I look for companies that sell non-genetically modified seeds and that offer lots of heirloom seed options. I also tend to stick to companies that are in my general climate range, as I hope that what's growing well in their test gardens will also thrive in mine. Look for catalogs that list the seed source, so you know whether the seed stock comes from a regional location or from as far away as Denmark. Because I like to grow a little bit of everything, I also keep an eye out for companies that offer smaller seed packet sizes with hopefully smaller prices, so I can justify my Noah's Ark approach to gardening.

Seed-Starting Dates:
Timing Is Everything

To figure out when to start your seeds, you need to know your last frost date. Your last frost date is not a green light to get your garden in the ground. Rather, it is an estimated date, based on decades of data, for when your region may experience the last dip in below-freezing temperatures for the season. Here in Zone 5b, our last frost date is usually May 2. But often the reality is that our soil on May 2 still has a lot of thawing to do before it's workable. You can find your frost dates by visiting the National Gardening Association's website (see Resources, page 235). Enter your zip code and you'll get specific information for your region.

Your last frost date usually signals that it is safe to plant hardened-off cool-weather crops like brassicas, lettuce, and onions. In many areas, you can start sowing peas, radishes, and spinach in the garden 4 to 6 weeks before your last frost date, as long as the soil is workable. It's also a good time to direct sow hardy annuals like alyssum, cornflowers, larkspur, and love-in-a-mist.

You'll want to wait for the soil to warm up before you transplant warm-weather crops like tomatoes, cucumbers, and squash, as well as tender annuals like zinnias, sunflowers, and coleus. It's also good to wait for warmer soil before you direct sow crops like beans and pumpkins. Memorial Day weekend traditionally serves as our start to these warm-weather plantings.

BIGGER ISN'T ALWAYS BETTER

You know those huge, hulking, happy seedlings that have overtaken your living room (those tomatoes you might have innocently started a few weeks earlier than the recommended 6, or those cosmos seedlings that are now forming flower buds)? Well, those seemingly advanced seedlings are going to need more time to adjust to their new digs before they can begin to focus on growing. Smaller seedlings, once transplanted, go straight into growing mode; within a few weeks, they can be indistinguishable in size from ones transplanted out as much larger seedlings. Exercise a bit of patience (so hard to do!) and stick to the recommended starting dates listed on your seed packets.

GROW

Sow Indoors or Out

Some seeds fare better sown directly into the ground, while others are better suited to being started indoors, then transplanted. Very simply put, start tender, heat-loving plants indoors and direct sow root crops and cold-hardy plants outdoors. Seeds that germinate quickly, like radishes and beans, are also ideal candidates for direct sowing. Crops like peas, beets, squash, spinach, nasturtiums, and snapdragons are not fans of transplanting, so they are best direct sown outside. If you do need to get a head start on these crops, then start them indoors in compostable containers that can be placed directly in the ground with the plants, so as to not to disturb the seedlings' roots.

DIRECT SEED OUTSIDE

Vegetables: beans, beets, carrots, chard, corn, cucumber*, lettuce*, peas, pumpkins*, radish, spinach, squash*, turnips

Herbs: calendula*, cilantro, dill

Flowers: Bells of Ireland*, larkspur*, love-in-a-mist, sunflowers*, zinnias*

* These plants may also be started indoors. See facing page.

START INDOORS

Vegetables: Brussels sprouts, broccoli, cabbage, cauliflower, eggplant, kale, leeks, onions, peppers, tomatoes

Herbs: basil, lavender, rosemary

Flowers: asters, cosmos, marigolds, pansies, violets

Plants with delicate roots:** celery, chard, cucumbers, melons, pumpkins, spinach, squash

** Start indoors in compostable containers.

Sow Those Seeds!

Now that you've determined your last frost date and which crops you'll start indoors, it's time to grab a calendar and a pen and count your way back from your last frost date to when your seed packet recommends starting indoors.

Start Indoors 10 to 12 Weeks before the Last Frost Date
Vegetables: celery, leeks, onions
Herbs: lavender, rosemary
Flowers: delphinium, echinacea, foxglove, petunia, sweet William, verbena, viola

Start Indoors 8 to 10 Weeks before the Last Frost Date
Vegetables: eggplant, peppers
Herbs: parsley
Flowers: dahlia, forget-me-not, hollyhock, impatiens, pansy, rudbeckia, snapdragon, statice, stock, yarrow

Start Indoors 6 to 8 Weeks before the Last Frost Date
Vegetables: tomatoes
Herbs: basil, catnip, calendula, lemon balm, oregano, sage, thyme, winter savory
Flowers: aster, balsam, bee balm, bells of Ireland, calendula, celosia, coleus, cornflower, gomphrena, larkspur, linaria, lupine, marigold, phlox, salvia, strawflower, sweet Annie

Start Indoors 4 to 6 Weeks before the Last Frost Date
Vegetables: broccoli, cabbage, cauliflower, kale
Herbs: chamomile
Flowers: alyssum, amaranth, cosmos, scabiosa, sweet pea, zinnia

Start Indoors 2 to 4 Weeks before the Last Frost Date
Vegetables: cucumbers, lettuce, melons, squash, pumpkins
Flowers: morning glory, nasturtium, sunflower

Direct Sow Outdoors 4 to 6 Weeks before the Last Frost Date
Vegetables: peas, radishes, spinach

Direct Sow Outdoors 2 to 4 Weeks before the Last Frost Date
Vegetables: beets, carrots

Direct Sow Outdoors 2 to 4 Weeks after the Last Frost Date
Vegetables: beans, corn, cucumbers, pumpkins, summer squash, winter squash, and tender herbs and annuals

Seed Viability

Before you place your seed order, take stock of any seed you already have from past seasons. You'll also want to check the seed's viability—its ability to germinate and grow. Even with a fresh packet, not every seed will germinate. As your carryover seed packets age, their germination rate drops. Let's say a brand-new seed has a 90 percent germination rate. That means 9 out of every 10 seeds sown should grow. Once that same seed is about 3 years old, the germination rate drops to around 60 percent; you'll need to sow more of those older seeds to ensure enough germination.

How Long Will My Seeds Last?

This list is an estimate. Many seeds are viable for longer, especially if stored properly, while some have a bit shorter shelf life. Do a quick viability test before planting older seed.

Herbs	Years
Anise	5
Basil	5–7
Calendula	3
Catnip	5
Chamomile	3
Chives	1
Cilantro	5–7
Dill	3
Fennel	4
Lavender	5
Oregano	2
Parsley	1
Sage	3
Savory	3
Thyme	3

Fruits & Vegetables	Years
Asparagus	3
Beans	3
Beet	4
Broccoli	4
Brussels sprouts	4
Cabbage	4
Carrot	3
Cauliflower	4
Celery	3
Chard, Swiss	4
Corn, sweet	2
Cucumber	5
Eggplant	4
Endive	5
Kale	4
Leek	2
Lettuce	4
Melon	5
Onion	1
Parsnip	1
Pea	3
Pepper	3

Fruits & Vegetables	Years
Pumpkin	4
Radish	4
Rutabaga	4
Spinach	2
Squash	4
Tomato	5
Turnip	4
Watermelon	4

Flowers	Years
Ageratum	4
Alyssum	4
Amaranth	4
Aster	1
Baby's breath	2
Bachelor's button	3
Calendula	5
Celosia	4
Clarkia	2
Coleus	2
Columbine	2
Cosmos	3
Dahlia	2
Daisy	3
Delphinium	1

Flowers	Years
Dianthus	4
Foxglove	2
Geranium	1
Hibiscus	3
Hollyhock	3
Impatiens	2
Larkspur	1
Lobelia	3
Lupine	2
Marigold	2
Nasturtium	5
Nicotiana	3
Pansy	2
Petunia	3
Phlox	1
Poppy	4
Salvia	1
Snapdragon	3
Sweet Pea	3
Verbena	1

BEFORE YOU SOW, KEY TERMS TO KNOW

While age, variety, and storage are key in determining a seed's ability to germinate, a few other factors can come into play.

Light. Some seeds need light to germinate, while others need darkness.

Presoaking and scarification. Some seeds have tough outer seed coats that are difficult for seedlings to break through. To soften that outer cover, you can pre-soak the seed overnight. You can also use sandpaper or a knife to gently scratch the seed coat, scarifying it—basically, creating an opening for the seedling to emerge through.

Cold treatment. Some seeds need to be exposed to a period of cold prior to being able to germinate. How cold and for how long depends on the plant, but most can just be placed in the refrigerator for a few weeks prior to sowing.

HOW TO

Do a Germination Test to Check Your Seed's Viability

1 Fold a dampened paper towel in half.

2 Take a few seeds and place them on the damp towel.

3 Fold the towel over the seeds and place in a plastic bag in a warm location.

4 After a few days, open the bag and peek to see what's germinated. That'll give you a good gauge of how your seeds are doing.

If the germination rate is low but there is still viability, simply sow those seeds at a heavier rate, knowing that not all will germinate.

Setting Up
Your Grow Station

What started for me as a simple shop light hanging over a shelf morphed into a dedicated shelf with four shop lights, which grew to be a couple of shelves with even more shop lights. Now I take over our dining room as my primary growing space. Like some funky art installation, more than a dozen shop lights hang at various heights ready to be choreographed to the seedlings' height as they grow. It's not pretty, nor is it small, but it works like a charm.

What You'll Need to Get Growing

Seedling containers to sow in. You can pretty much grow in anything if it is clean and sterile and offers drainage.

Seed-starting mix. Use quality seed-starting mix—or make your own. But sow larger seeds like pumpkin and sunflower directly into potting soil mix, which better supports the larger seeds.

Trays. These hold seedlings and collect any water.

Humidity covers for the trays. You can purchase specifically designed humidity domes, but plastic bags work just as well. I slide the bags over the seedling containers and remove after germination.

Warmth. Many seeds need heat to germinate. A warming mat is an option, or you can place trays on top of your refrigerator (my preferred method).

Good lighting. If you are blessed with endless sunshine pouring through your windows all day long, you can probably put seedlings on your windowsill. But for those of us living in semidarkness this time of year, grow lights are a must. There are many different options out there, with different types of bulbs. For all the details, see Choosing the Right Light (at right).

Shelving. Seedlings grow (well, hopefully!), so keep that in mind when setting up your shelving system. You'll need to be able to either raise the shelves toward the light or drop the light down toward the shelf. You'll want to keep the lights 2 to 4 inches above the seedlings as they grow (higher as they get larger).

If you need to keep "helpful" kitties or young ones at bay, use some kind of screen to fence off your indoor growing area. A roll of window screening works great, or even a lightweight shower curtain.

CHOOSING THE RIGHT LIGHT

Your options for grow lights can run the gamut from a basic shop light to a full-blown light stand. Before you invest in a lighting setup, however, figure out what best fits your growing needs. If you're new to gardening and simply want to start seedlings indoors for spring planting, then beginning with a simple shop light that holds two 40-watt T12 fluorescent bulbs is best. Make sure you have one cool bulb and one warm bulb. You can hang this setup from your ceiling or rig it to hang on a shelf unit.

LED lights are a great option if you know you'll use them for the next several years. They are a bigger up-front investment, but one that will pay off over time. LED plant lights offer a full spectrum of light, including blue light, which promotes the chlorophyll and leaf production in leafy vegetables and herbs, and red light, which benefits blossom production in flowering or fruiting plants. LED lights come in different shape options, from large overhead hanging ones (best for taller seedlings like tomatoes) to tabletop models. You can also create a balance by using a combination of both red and blue lights.

When choosing between types of light, factor in your setup space. LED lights need to hang at least 14 to 24 inches above the plants. In contrast, fluorescent lights can hang as little as 3 inches above the plants, making it easy to hang several shop lights on one stacked shelving unit.

Milk Jug Winter Sowing

A lot of flower seeds are best direct sown in early spring "as soon as soil can be worked," as many people say. That can be a tricky window to catch, especially here in Maine, where we can go from winter to a week or two of spring then straight into summer.

In the past, it's been more miss than hit with my attempts at indoor sowing these seeds as well as directly sowing them in early May, when our soil has finally thawed. While both methods resulted in blooms, the plants themselves were just okay. It wasn't until I sowed these same seeds using the milk jug method that I witnessed how huge, lush, and prolific these flowers truly can be. Think of this method as maintenance-free mini greenhouse growing, where all you have to do is prep the container, sow the seeds, and then just set it outside until spring rolls around and you spy seedlings growing inside.

There are several benefits to sowing in these powerful "greenhouses in disguise."

✳ Many flowers with recommended early-spring sowings require stratification—which is exposure to cold—to germinate. This method of sowing does exactly that.

✳ The milk jug method saves you valuable growing room indoors. Think of all the room you'll have under those grow lights to experiment with some new seeds as other seeds sit happily outside.

✳ It's maintenance-free. No tending needed.

✳ Nature takes care of the hardening-off process.

✳ Plants grown in this method are acclimated to the local climate so that they focus purely on growing rather than adjusting to their environment.

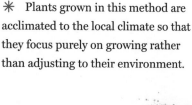

MAKE

Milk Jug Mini Greenhouses

1 Collect some clean milk jugs and poke several drainage holes in the bottom of each.

2 Starting around the base of the handle, cut the jug horizontally across, stopping short to leave a 2-inch connected segment, which will act as a hinge.

3 Dampen the potting mix and fill the bottom half of the milk jug. Gently pat down the mix. Sow seeds to the depth and light specified by the seed packet.

4 Flip back the top half of the jug to close it over the bottom half. Using duct tape, seal the seam shut.

You can toss the milk jug cap; you'll want to keep that off, to allow rain to enter and excess heat to escape. Place your jugs in a sunny location. I nestle mine right into the snowbank along the south end of our house. Check on them occasionally. As spring begins to warm up, they may need some water so that the potting mix doesn't dry out. As soon as your garden soil is ready, remove the tape from the jugs and gently transplant your seedlings.

FALSE QUEEN ANNE'S LACE

CORNFLOWERS

POPPIES

Favorite Flowers to Start with the MILK JUG METHOD

False Queen Anne's lace
Bells of Ireland
Clarkia
Cornflowers
Larkspur
Love-in-a-mist
Poppies
Scabiosa
Snapdragon
Sweet peas

LARKSPUR

SNAPDRAGONS

LOVE-IN-A-MIST

PUMPKINS, WINTER SQUASH & GOURDS

If you want to grow happiness, grow pumpkins, winter squash, and gourds. Not only will these plants delight and amaze you in the garden, but their bounty will bring joy for the indoor months to come. When the days of garden freshness have long passed, being able to feast on one of your own squashes in the depths of December feels pretty incredible. It tastes incredible, too! One of my favorite things to do with these whimsical orbs is to keep the garden spirit bright by displaying them throughout the house.

WHEN TO SOW
Direct sow a few weeks after the last frost date, once the soil has warmed.

SOIL
Compost-rich, well-drained soil

PREFERRED LIGHT
Full sun

Tips + Tricks

- Before sowing, use a nail file or sandpaper to gently rub the edges of the seed to aid in germination.

- Help ease transplant shock by sowing squash seeds started indoors into containers that can be directly planted into the garden.

- Direct sow outdoors, three or four seeds in a cluster on a mound.

- Save space and grow perfect fruits by growing vertically. Plant smaller pumpkins, squash, and gourds to climb up trellises or archways, which not only maximizes precious growing space but also keeps the fruits from sitting on the ground and thus helps prevent blemishes and rotting.

- Plant along the garden's edges so vines have room to sprawl.

- Provide these heavy feeders with a big helping of compost in each sowing spot. When fruits begin to set, give a feeding of fertilizer.

- Keep well watered, but make sure to avoid watering from above because that can encourage powdery mildew to develop.

- Firmly pat down the soil around the base of the plant, and/or place a protective aluminum foil collar (made from a 15-inch square of foil) shiny side up around the base of the stem to ward off squash vine borers.

- Harvest once the skin cannot be easily pierced by a fingernail, making sure to leave a 2- to 3-inch stem attached.

Get all the squash and none of the sprawl by growing compact varieties like 'Butterscotch PMR', 'Honeynut', 'Sweet Dumpling', 'Gold Nugget', and 'Burpee's Butterbush'.

Favorite Varieties

There are so many incredible and unique varieties to explore! Have fun and try several, to find out which ones thrive where you grow. Northern gardeners, pay close attention to the number of days needed for the squash to fully ripen, and look for varieties that are on the shorter spectrum of days, to add a buffer in case of early frost. Squash that aren't fully ripe won't store well.

WINTER SQUASH: 'Baby Blue Hubbard', 'Waltham Butternut', 'Delicata'

PUMPKINS: 'Casperita', 'Lumina', 'Howden', 'New England Pie', 'Jarrahdale', 'Jack-Be-Little'

GOURDS: 'Tennessee Dancing', 'Small Warted Mix'

BUTTERNUT SQUASH
AND DELICATA

WARTY GOURD

'TENNESSEE DANCING' GOURD

'HOWDEN' PUMPKIN

Storing Tips

Prepare squash for long-term storage by properly curing it. Curing simply allows excess moisture to dissipate, aiding in extending the squash's shelf life. After harvest, set the squash and pumpkins on racks in a warm location with good air circulation and leave them there for 2 weeks. Before storing away, wipe down each squash and pumpkin with a diluted vinegar solution (about one part vinegar to four parts water) to remove any bacteria and possible mold inducers and keep your precious harvest going until you sow the seeds for next year's crop. Store in a location that stays between 50 and 55°F with 50–70% relative humidity.

AS THE GOURD TURNS

The first time I grew a trellis of ornamental gourds, it was love at first sight. But I convinced myself that the gourds couldn't earn a place in the following year's garden because I needed that precious growing space for veggies—something we could eat. But during that gourdless season, their absence left a noticeable void. Since then, gourds of all sorts of shapes and sizes have rambled about my garden. These lovelies will adorn our Thanksgiving Day table as centerpieces as well as place settings. A few will even provide after-dinner entertainment when we start spinning the tiny 'Tennessee Dancing' gourds like tops across the table. Come December, when I must rationalize why I still have dozens of gourds hanging about, I'll paint a few silver and tuck others into holiday displays.

EAT

PUMPKIN–CHOCOLATE CHIP MUFFINS

Not all pumpkins are equal when it comes to eating quality. For best baking results, use pie pumpkins.

MAKES 12 MUFFINS

1 cup pumpkin puree	1 teaspoon baking soda
¾ cup sugar	¾ teaspoon baking powder
½ cup vegetable oil	½ teaspoon salt
2 eggs	½ teaspoon nutmeg
1 teaspoon vanilla extract	1½ cups chocolate chips
1½ cups all-purpose flour	

1 Preheat the oven to 400°F/200°C. Grease and flour a muffin pan or use paper liners.

2 Mix together the pumpkin, sugar, oil, eggs, and vanilla in a large bowl. Combine the flour, baking soda, baking powder, salt, and nutmeg in a medium bowl. Add the flour mixture to the pumpkin mixture and fold together until just combined. Gently fold in the chocolate chips.

3 Spoon the batter evenly into the prepared muffin cups. Bake for 15 to 18 minutes. Cool in the pan for a few minutes, then transfer the muffins to a wire rack.

4 Store in an airtight container for up to 5 days or freeze for up to 3 months.

A Winter-Weather Treat for Chickens

Hens can be a bunch of chickens when it comes to winter's frosty white stuff. Either they don't dare dip a toe, or they fearfully fly out into it, then panic like they're stranded on a deserted island. Some hens just don't like snow, but I think that for many, the snow toys with their sense of depth perception, making them unsure of where to step. So we sprinkle hay on top of the snow whenever shoveling out the chicken run isn't possible (this snow is basically rock-hard ice). As soon as the birds see the hay, they happily strut on out of the coop. And to keep them milling about outside in the cold instead of racing back inside, we ply them with warm nibbles of roasted garden winter squash stuffed with seeds and oats. Once the squash is reduced to empty shells, then the chickens race back into the warmth of the coop, but at least they got outside for a bit.

AMERAUCANA

AMERAUCANAS

AMERAUCANA CHICKS

Favorite CHICKEN BREEDS

Late winter is a popular time to order chicks either at a local farmers' co-op or with a breeder online. Over the past 12 years, we've raised several different breeds of hens. Here in Maine, we look for cold-hardy breeds with short combs/wattles. Wyandottes (Silver and Golden Laced), Barred Rock, Buff Orpingtons, and Ameraucanas have been our favorite breeds, both for hardiness and personality.

DOUBLE SILVER LACED BARNEVELDER

LIGHT BRAHMAS

DRIED BEANS

*Grab your dried pods and a bowl.
Put on a good movie, grab a nice drink,
and start shelling those pods.*

WHEN TO SOW
Direct sow once the soil
has warmed.

SOIL Well-drained soil

PREFERRED LIGHT
Full sun

Tips + Tricks

GROWING

- Avoid fertilizing with too much nitrogen: That encourages more leaf growth than pod development. Instead, apply an inoculant when sowing seed. An inoculant is a type of rhizobium bacteria that helps fix nitrogen for the plant and aids in its growth.

- Reduce watering in the 2 weeks leading up to harvesttime and plan to harvest during periods of dry weather.

HARVESTING

- Wait to harvest until the pods are brown and burgeoning. The plant's foliage will be yellowed and withered. You should hear the beans rattle in the pods.

- After picking, let the pods hang out in a cool, dry place out of direct sunlight for a few weeks so that they dry completely before shelling.

USING

- Store in jars for winter eating or spring sowing—or both!

- Be totally sure that no insects have stowed away in your beans by placing the jar in the freezer for a week before storing it in your pantry. The freezing temperatures will kill any critters.

Favorite Varieties

'Jacob's Cattle', 'Vermont Cranberry Pole',
'Tiger's Eye', 'King of the Early'

MAPLE BAKED BEANS

This is my family's favorite way to celebrate the first batch of maple syrup. Each March, we mix up a big batch of these beans in a Dutch oven and let it simmer alongside the sap that's boiling down for our next round of syrup. It's a slow, all-day cook that results in the slightly sweet yet subtle flavor of maple happiness.

SERVES 10–12

1	pound dried beans (your choice), rinsed then soaked overnight
1	teaspoon salt
1	large onion, diced
3	garlic cloves, diced
4	bacon strips, diced
1	cup maple syrup
¼	cup ketchup
2	teaspoons dry mustard
½	teaspoon cracked black pepper

1 Drain the soaked beans and put them in a large saucepan. Cover the beans with enough water to fully submerge them, stir in the salt, and bring to a boil. Reduce the heat to low, cover the pot, and simmer until tender, about 2 hours.

2 Preheat the oven to 325°F/170°C.

3 Strain the beans, reserving the cooking liquid. In a 3-quart Dutch oven or oven-safe pot, layer the beans, onion, garlic, and bacon.

4 Combine the maple syrup, ketchup, mustard, and pepper in a small bowl and mix well. Pour the mixture over the beans. Add enough of the reserved cooking liquid, or boiling water, to cover the beans by ½ inch.

5 Cover and bake for 3 to 3½ hours. Check the liquid level of the pot occasionally. If the beans are looking dry, add a bit of boiling water. If they're too soupy, remove the lid during the last hour of the bake.

RUNNER BEANS: THERE'S MAGIC INSIDE THAT POD

These beautiful pole beans are pure eye candy in the garden, flushing trellises and archways in a carpet of heart-shaped green leaves dotted with stunning, edible red flowers that endlessly beckon hummingbirds and make salads sparkle. Every stage of growing these beautiful beans is a celebration unto itself.

◆ They germinate quickly for instant gratification.

◆ They twine clockwise as they're growing, whereas pole beans go counterclockwise.

◆ Just as the hummingbirds begin their constant hover, the pods begin to appear—one after another, month after month, hanging like gorgeous veggie ornaments waiting to be plucked.

◆ When picked young, the pods can be eaten whole, much like you would any green bean. If you wait to harvest them as a shell bean, avoid consuming large quantities of the raw beans, as they contain a toxin that could cause digestive discomfort (you would have to eat an immense amount to get more ill than that). When cooked thoroughly, the toxin is removed.

◆ Let them dry on the vine, and you'll find the unassuming browning pods hold the prettiest treasures inside. When used as a dried bean, they're lovely in stews, casseroles, and chili.

WINTER

KALE & FRIENDS: THE BRASSICA FAMILY

Often the key to bounties of brassicas is sowing the right variety at the right time. Broccoli varieties vary from early to mid- to long season. I like to guarantee myself season-long noshing by growing a few plants of each of the different seasonal varieties, with 'Arcadia' and 'Di Cicco' as my early-season favorites and 'Belstar' and 'Waltham 29' as my midseason picks, followed by later-to-harvest varieties like 'Romanesco' and 'Purple Sprouting'. Some crops like Brussels sprouts and cauliflower fare much better when planted as fall crops rather than spring.

WHEN TO SOW
Start indoors 6 to 8 weeks before the last frost date.

SOIL Moist, well-drained, compost-rich soil

PREFERRED LIGHT
Full sun

Favorite Varieties

BROCCOLI:
'Windsor', 'Arcadia', 'Belstar'

KALE:
'Toscano', 'Winterbor', 'Red Russian'

CABBAGE:
'Ruby Perfection', 'Early Jersey Wakefield', 'Red Acre'

Tips + Tricks

GROWING

- Companion plant cabbage and kale with chamomile, sage, mint (in a pot), and dill. Mint gives brassicas a flavor boost. Sage wards off the small white butterfly that lays the cabbageworms.

- Eat your landscape. Kale and cabbage are not only good-for-you veggies, they are gorgeous additions to any garden design, offering dozens of different hues, textures, and shapes that only get more stunning as the season chugs along. When planning your garden layout, think beyond harvesting for dinner and ponder the possibilities brassicas can bring to the visual presentation of your garden.

- Keep your brassicas content by mulching with grass or straw so that the soil stays a bit cooler and the plants' roots are moist.

HARVESTING

- Harvest kale from the outside in, leaving the center leaves intact so the plant will keep growing.

USING

- Dehydrate the leaves from bumper harvests of kale to make your own superfood powder for shakes. Once the leaves are cracker-dry, all you have to do is grind and go.

- Nutritional fast facts: Red cabbage has twice the amount of vitamin C as green cabbage. Unlike a lot of veggies, kale doesn't lose any of its nutritional mojo when cooked.

'WINDSOR' BROCCOLI

'RED ACRE' CABBAGE

Kale was such a favorite vegetable in Scotland that the saying "Come to kale" was meant as an invitation to dinner.

'WINTERBOR' KALE

Ways to Keep Your Brassicas Pest-Free

✳ **Collar those brassica babies.** Cut a 6-inch square of cardboard, tar paper, or other stiff paper and fit it snugly around the base of the plant. This protects the base of the stem where cabbage maggot flies like to lay their eggs.

✳ **Stomp in your transplants.** This sounds nutty, but by applying full body weight gently but firmly around the base of a transplanted seedling, you make a tight soil seal around the neck of the seedling, so the cabbage maggot fly can't easily lay its eggs there.

✳ **Time your planting.** Avoid transplanting seedlings into the garden during hatching time.

✳ **Use row covers.** To set up row covers in the garden, install a series of hoops over the bed—bent PVC conduit works well—and clip the row cover material to the hoops. Trying to spread row cover over straight poles will wear holes in the material, and even the smallest hole can let the flies in.

✳ **Watch your rotation.** Never use row cover on a bed that grew cucurbits the previous season. The flies can overwinter in the soil, so covering that soil with row cover actually traps the bugs in, creating their ideal environment to hatch, match, and lay eggs.

✳ **Till in fall; till in spring.** Cabbage maggot flies stay within the top 5 inches of soil. By tilling deeply at the end and beginning of gardening seasons, you disrupt the maggot's life cycle.

COMPANION PLANTING WITH CABBAGE

Cabbages make such a gorgeous statement in the garden that it feels almost unbearable to harvest one and rob the landscape of its beauty. And because of their unbridled gorgeousness, I can never bring myself to cover them with row covers to protect them from cabbage worm foes. So I practice companion planting instead. Not only will partner plants like dill, chamomile, and sage help protect your cabbage crop, they will also create a dynamic garden design. Interplanting veggies, herbs, and flowers adds instant whimsy and interest.

EAT

MASSAGE YOUR KALE

Although I love kale's toughness when it comes to tolerating cold temperatures, that same attribute can make the vegetable harder to chew. Kale's fibrous leaves soften when cooked, but when eaten fresh, they could use a hand—literally. Massaging kale leaves with a dressing of your choice helps tenderize those tough leaves: The acids from the vinegar and/or lemon juice in the dressing help break down kale's fibrous texture, making the leaves much more tender.

To begin, cut the leaves away from the stem and tear into bite-size pieces. Using your fingers, massage the kale and dressing together until the leaves just begin to wilt. Let sit for 10 minutes. Finish making your salad and start feasting.

HOW TO
Store Your Broccoli

DITCH THE PLASTIC. Did you know broccoli needs to breathe? Broccoli releases ethylene, and that gas gets trapped when the broccoli is sealed tight, which hastens the breakdown of your precious veggie. So please don't suffocate it by zipping it into a sealed container. Rather, loosely wrap the unwashed broccoli heads in a damp paper towel. They should keep crisp and fresh in the fridge for 3 to 5 days. You can also store broccoli like you would asparagus—fill a jar partway with water, plop in your broccoli bouquet, and stash it in the fridge.

BLANCH AND FREEZE FLORETS. If you have a few minutes to spare, prep your broccoli now for feasting later by freezing it. Separate the heads into florets. Blanch in boiling water for 3 minutes, then immerse immediately in an ice water bath for 3 minutes. Dry the florets thoroughly and store in an airtight container in the freezer. Alternatively, spread out the washed and dried broccoli onto a baking sheet and flash freeze for a few hours before storing in a container. This second method makes it easy to gather a handful of frozen florets rather than a broccoli iceberg.

EAT
ROASTED BRUSSELS SPROUTS

One of my proudest skills as a cook is my ability to convert a Brussels sprouts hater into a lover after their first bite of a roasted sprout. Suddenly, these formerly rejected green orbs become the new enthusiast's most-requested dish. Even better, Brussels sprouts can be ready for roasting in mere minutes.

Preheat the oven to 425°F/220°C. Wash and dry the Brussels sprouts. If they're on the larger side, cut them in half. Peel off the outer layer of leaves. Toss the sprouts onto a baking sheet and drizzle them with olive oil, sea salt, and freshly ground black pepper. Using your hands, massage the sprouts with the oil until they are thoroughly coated. Roast for 35 to 45 minutes, giving them a toss halfway through the baking time.

WINTER

213

WINTER SAVORY

Winter savory is a hardy, bushy perennial whose peppery flavor pairs perfectly with beans, roasts, stuffings, and stews.

WHEN TO SOW Start indoors 6 to 8 weeks before the last frost date.

SOIL Well-drained soil

PREFERRED LIGHT Full sun

Tips + Tricks

GROWING

◆ Use as a companion plant near any crops that are battling aphids or bean weevils. Winter savory acts as a deterrent to those pests.

◆ Propagate this slow-to-germinate herb by stem cuttings to get a leg up on the growing game.

◆ Prune back in spring to encourage bushiness.

◆ Grow an aromatic herbal hedge in front borders by planting winter savory along with thyme, lavender, and sage.

◆ Let your savory go to flower once you have harvested your fill of it, and you'll be thanked by pollinators of all sorts.

EATING

◆ Use as a substitute for thyme in a pinch.

TARRAGON

Known as the "king of herbs" in France, this tall perennial is still making a name for itself stateside. Its concentrated anise flavor is so powerful that a little goes a long way. When setting it out in the garden, keep in mind that this gangly herb likes room to sprawl.

WHEN TO SOW
Start plants from cuttings.

SOIL Rich, well-drained soil

PREFERRED LIGHT
Full sun

Tips + Tricks

GROWING

- Propagate this hardy perennial from cuttings; its seeds are sterile.
- Plant toward the back of a bed and provide support to keep this gangly herb from flopping.
- Divide the plant every 3 to 5 years.

USING

- Dry now for use later. Unlike most tender herbs, whose flavor tends to fade quickly once dried, tarragon's flavor not only lasts but becomes more concentrated.
- Add it to your favorite chicken, egg, and seafood dishes.

TASTE BEFORE BUYING

Taste your tarragon plant before bringing it home. Tarragon is one of the most mislabeled herbs sold in nurseries. Often, Russian tarragon is sold in place of the more desired French tarragon. Both plants look similar, with Russian being a bit taller. The true difference is in the taste and the tingle. French tarragon has an anise flavor that leaves a tinge of a tingle on your tongue after chewing it. You may also come across Mexican tarragon, which can be a good substitute taste-wise, but avoid the Russian varieties. They offer no taste for culinary use.

EAT
TARRAGON VINEGAR

Put tarragon's flavor in the spotlight by making an infused vinegar. For maximum flavor, harvest the tarragon early in its season, and early in the morning.

MAKES 2 CUPS

1 cup tarragon sprigs, gently rinsed and patted completely dry
2 cups white wine vinegar

1 If desired, set aside 1 tarragon sprig for later decorative use. Place the remaining sprigs in a sterilized jar. Using a wooden spoon, gently bruise the tarragon. Completely cover the herb with vinegar.

2 Put on a plastic or other nonreactive lid and let the mixture steep in a cool, dark place for 2 weeks so that the flavors infuse, giving the jar an easy shake every few days.

3 Strain the vinegar, discard the tarragon, and pour the finished vinegar into a sterilized bottle. If desired, add the reserved tarragon sprig to the jar. Store in a cool, dark place for up to 6 months.

PARSLEY

Parsley is a rewarding herb to start from seed. It's slow to start, but once it gets going, it grows quickly. In a short amount of time, you'll find yourself with bushy plants full of bright, fresh flavor.

WHEN TO SOW Start indoors 8 to 10 weeks before the last frost date.

SOIL Compost-rich, well-drained soil

PREFERRED LIGHT Full to part sun

Tips + Tricks

- Companion plant with asparagus, beans, brassicas, corn, peppers, and tomatoes.

- Grow this biennial herb as an annual for best results. Parsley is quick to bolt in its second year of growth.

- Sow extra seeds to bolster your success rate for this herb, which is notorious for its low and slow germination rate.

- Avoid transplant shock by sowing in compostable pots that can be directly planted into the ground come late spring.

- Keep well watered during the hottest days of summer.

- Be the butterfly host with the most. Parsley acts as a host plant for the caterpillars that become swallowtail butterflies.

Kitchen Tips

- For best flavor, grow the flat-leaf varieties. The curly variety is often sidelined on the dinner plate as a garnish more than a tasty meal addition.

- After harvesting, dry and wash the sprigs. Loosely roll them in a tea towel or in paper towels and place in a resealable plastic bag for up to a week. Or place freshly cut stalks in a jar of water and store in the refrigerator.

- Don't simply compost the stems; toss them into the freezer and use later to flavor stocks and soups.

- The roots are edible; use them as you would a carrot.

NOURISH

PARSLEY FACIAL TONER

This toner is refreshing, invigorating, and antiseptic. Pulse together ¼ cup chopped fresh parsley leaves, ¼ teaspoon witch hazel, and 2 tablespoons water in a food processor or blender. Strain out the solids through a fine-mesh sieve or cheesecloth and transfer the liquid to a bottle. Makes 4 ounces.

EAT

CHIMICHURRI SAUCE

This South American staple makes a zesty marinade or a vibrant tableside condiment for dipping and drizzling.

MAKES 8–12 OUNCES

1	cup fresh parsley
1	onion, thinly sliced
2	garlic cloves
¼	cup olive oil
¼	cup water
1	tablespoon lime juice
1	teaspoon distilled white vinegar
	Pinch of sugar
	Salt and freshly ground black pepper

Place the parsley, onion, garlic, oil, water, lime juice, vinegar, and sugar in a food processor and blend until smooth. Season with salt and pepper. Drizzle the sauce over veggies, fish, or meat. To preserve, freeze in ice cube trays.

PARSLEY-WALNUT PESTO

This is the perfect pesto to brighten a winter's day. Toss with pasta, stir into soups, spread on bread, or slather on roasted veggies.

MAKES 8–12 OUNCES

1	cup tightly packed fresh parsley
⅓	cup toasted walnuts
2	garlic cloves, smashed
¼	cup grated Parmesan cheese
¼	teaspoon lemon zest
1	tablespoon lemon juice
¼	cup extra-virgin olive oil
	Salt and freshly ground black pepper

Combine the parsley, nuts, garlic, Parmesan, lemon zest, and lemon juice in a food processor. Pulse for about 10 seconds. With the machine running, slowly add the oil in a steady stream until a paste forms. Season with salt and pepper. Keep the pesto in an airtight container in the refrigerator for up to 5 days.

WINTER

217

ROSEMARY

Rosemary is a wunderkind herb: It amps up the flavor in any dish, its aromatics help to promote a sense of calm, and it's easy to preserve. Whether in a patch or a pot, rosemary is sure to add instant joy to any garden.

WHEN TO SOW
Sow indoors 12 weeks before your last frost date.

SOIL Well-drained, sandy soil

PREFERRED LIGHT
Full sun

Medicinal Properties

Rich source of antioxidants; antibacterial, anti-inflammatory, antiviral, antifungal, analgesic

Tips + Tricks

GROWING

- Northern growers will need to grow their rosemary as an annual because these tender, woody perennials, native to the Mediterranean coast, do not like overwintering in cold climates.

- Avoid high humidity and overwatering, as both can lead to root rot.

- Grow the variety 'Arp' in cool climates.

- Rosemary's pungent aroma repels not only mosquitoes and flies but cabbage moths as well, so plant it near your favorite brassica.

- Pot up in 6- to 8-inch-deep containers with a slow-release fertilizer and keep close to your kitchen for easy access.

HARVESTING

- Harvest often to encourage more compact, bushier growth.

USING

- Toss rosemary's edible flowers into teas, dressings, salads, and baked goods.

- Get your daily vitamins' worth with each bite. Rosemary leaves are chock-full of volatile oils, flavonoids, vitamins A and C, and a whole host of minerals, including calcium, potassium, magnesium, and zinc.

- Promote a sense of well-being and calmness: This herb's medicinal properties aid in stress and anxiety relief. Rosemary also improves memory and mental clarity by increasing blood flow to the brain.

Harvesting Rosemary

Drying. To dry, hang stems upside down out of direct light in a room with good air circulation and low humidity. Don't tie stems together too tightly, as mold can grow if there is no airflow. Dry smaller stems on screens or racks.

Freezing. Rosemary preserves well by freezing. Just chop it, place it in an ice cube tray, cover with olive oil, and freeze. Or try flash freezing by placing rosemary leaves in one layer on a baking sheet and freezing for 20 to 30 minutes. Store in an airtight container in the freezer.

GLOSSY LOCKS ROSEMARY HAIR RINSE

This restorative rinse will banish the winter blahs from your hair and bring a little shine back in. Fill a clean jar halfway with a mix of dried chopped rosemary and mint leaves. Pour vinegar over the herbs, to the top inch of the jar. Place the jar in a warm spot, out of direct light, for 3 to 4 weeks. Give the mixture a gentle shake every few days. When ready, strain out the herbs and bottle the liquid. If you want, add a few drops of your favorite essential oil. Use after shampooing. Rinse with warm water, then finish with cold for extra gloss.

ROSEMARY & MINT HAIR OIL

Rosemary is a wonderful herb to use on your hair. It not only helps keep grays at bay by fighting off free radicals, thus slowing the color change, but it also gives curly hair good love by helping curls retain their shine; it nourishes the scalp and aids in eliminating flakes; and it adds instant gloss.

- 1 cup coconut oil
- 1 cup olive oil
- ½ cup dried rosemary leaves
- ½ cup dried peppermint leaves
- ½ cup dried calendula flowers

Combine the oils, leaves, and flowers in a glass jar and place on a sunny windowsill for 4 to 6 weeks. Alternatively, place all the ingredients in a double-boiler and slowly infuse for 4 to 6 hours over medium-low heat. After either infusion method, strain out the herbs and bottle the oil.

Use this hair oil as a preshampoo treatment: Warm it, apply it to the hair, and leave it on for 5 minutes before shampooing. Or use it to tame the frizzes (especially helpful for those with dry, curly, or wavy hair) or to protect your hair prior to blow-drying.

Note: Rosemary is great for brown hair. If your hair is blond, I recommend swapping out the rosemary for chamomile, which helps brighten lighter-hued locks.

SAGE

Ancient Romans used it to treat sore throats. Greeks use it to preserve meats. In traditional Chinese medicine, it is prescribed to increase mental capacity. Indigenous peoples traditionally used it to treat their skin. Let's just say, sage has been around the block a few times and has a lot to offer both in and outside the kitchen.

WHEN TO SOW Sow indoors 6 to 8 weeks before your last frost date.

SOIL Well-drained, sandy soil

PREFERRED LIGHT Full sun

Tips + Tricks

GROWING

- ◆ Companion plant with brassicas, calendula, carrots, and tomatoes; it will boost their growth. Avoid planting by cucumbers.
- ◆ Plant this woody perennial in partial shade if you're gardening in a very hot climate.
- ◆ Add pebbles around the base of the plant if you live in a damp climate. The pebbles help improve drainage, which aids in preventing mildew.
- ◆ Start indoors 6 to 8 weeks before last frost. It's easy to grow from seed.
- ◆ Prune sage in late spring by cutting out the oldest growth.
- ◆ Plant with rosemary, as both herbs seem to bolster each other's growth. Avoid planting it near basil, because they are more foes than friends.

HARVESTING

- ◆ Harvest lightly the first year to allow the plant time to get established.
- ◆ Harvest and dry the flower stems. Stems of sage leaves and flowers make fetching dried flowers that can be used in botanical wreaths and other crafts.

Medicinal Properties

Antibacterial, anti-inflammatory, antiseptic, antispasmodic, antioxidant

How Sage Heals

- Is rich in beta-carotene, vitamins B and C, calcium, iron, and magnesium

- Is a relaxant, helping to ease anxiety and stress

- Improves memory and sharpens senses; partner with rosemary for a double dose of this goodness

- Helps remove excess mucus in airways

- Reduces muscle tension and swelling

- Promotes restful sleep

- Stimulates digestion

- Soothes eczema

- Contains antioxidants that help reverse fine lines and wrinkles by protecting against skin-damaging free radicals

- Stimulates daily cell regeneration

NOURISH

SAGE SORE THROAT SOOTHER

All you need is 1 tablespoon of this mix swirled in tea to soothe a scratchy throat and calm a cough. Fill a sterilized glass jar halfway with finely chopped fresh sage. (You can use dried sage, but fresh tastes better.) Pour raw honey over the herbs, up to ½ inch from the top of the jar. Use a bamboo skewer to gently pop any air bubbles. Cover the jar and let sit in a cool, dark place for 1 month. Strain out the sage and pour the honey into a clean glass jar. Store at room temperature.

SAGE & LEMON BALM BODY POLISH

Scrub away those winter blues and reward your skin with polishing pleasure. Turns out, sugar is actually good for your body—at least when you use it as a gentle skin exfoliator. The granules release clogged pores and remove dead cells, leaving moisturized, glowing skin.

MAKES 16 OUNCES

1½	cups sugar
½	cup Epsom salts
1	cup almond oil
2	tablespoons ground lemon peel
1	tablespoon honey
2	teaspoons crushed dried lemon balm
1½	teaspoons crushed dried sage
1	teaspoon baking soda
6	drops lemon essential oil
8	drops sage essential oil
1	teaspoon vitamin E oil (optional; for longer-term preservation)

1 Mix together the sugar, salts, oil, lemon peel, honey, lemon balm, and sage in a large bowl.

2 Put the baking soda in a small bowl. Add the essential oils and thoroughly incorporate. (Doing this helps evenly distribute the essential oils throughout the body polish.)

3 Stir the baking soda mixture into the sugar mixture and add the vitamin E oil, if using. Transfer to a glass container and keep in a cool spot out of direct sun.

HOW TO

Harvest & Dry Sage

Cut the fresh, lighter green outer leaves, leaving the woodier stems to encourage bushier plants. Gather in small bundles and hang them upside down in a well-ventilated, dry location for about 2 weeks. Once the bundles are brittle to the touch, store them in airtight containers, keeping the leaves whole and crushing only when needed.

Sage Tea

If you want extra soothing, try swirling sage-infused honey in a cup of sage tea. A few sips of this brew work wonders for taking the scratch out of sore throats, and it can also help relieve cramps and hot flashes.

Put 1 to 2 teaspoons of dried sage leaves or 8 to 10 fresh leaves in a cup. Pour 1 cup boiling water over the leaves. Cover the cup to trap the precious essential oils. Let steep for 10 minutes. Slowly remove the cover and breathe in the uplifting sage steam. Add honey or lemon to taste. Also try adding other herbs like lemon verbena, mint, or thyme to your tea blend.

Warning: Pregnant and nursing moms should avoid sage, as it can dry up milk production.

223

Maple sugaring is my favorite winter pastime while waiting for flowers to grow.

The Joys of Maple Syrup Season

This is the sweetest time of the year! Come late February, when daytime temperatures begin to warm yet the nights still fall below freezing, it's time to tap the sugar maple trees—and maple syrup season officially begins. A short drive along our road illustrates the popularity of sugaring season in our region. Some homes have beautiful old galvanized sap buckets collecting sap. Other places, like ours, use whatever clean bucketlike item we can find, which is usually a juice or water jug.

Did you know that it takes 40 gallons of sap to make 1 gallon of maple syrup? And to make that gallon of syrup, you have to spend almost an entire day boiling down the sap and use a huge amount of wood to keep the fire stoked. Before we started making our own syrup, I used to cringe at the cost of real maple syrup. Now when I see it I think, "What a bargain!" In our house, maple syrup is like liquid gold—nary a drop of this priceless treat goes to waste.

You Can Tap More Than Sugar Maples

You can make syrup from any maple tree—including red, silver, Norway, black, and bigleaf. The biggest difference when tapping species other than sugar maples is that they have a much lower sugar content. That means you'll need to collect more sap from these trees than you would from a sugar maple; the ratio of sap to sugar is more like 60:1 compared with sugar maple's 40:1. Sugar content varies by species, so do a bit of research, and experiment to see which species will work for you.

Every few years, we tap our birch trees for their delicious sweetness, but to make 1 gallon of syrup, we would need to collect 100 gallons of sap! Instead, we usually make a pint of birch syrup, which proves to be more than plenty to enjoy. And for folks who have butternut trees nearby, I've heard that those trees make a delicious syrup and that you need only 20 to 30 gallons of their sap to craft 1 gallon of syrup!

Here are a few trees perfect for tapping.

- ✳ Bigleaf maple
- ✳ Black maple
- ✳ Norway maple
- ✳ Red maple
- ✳ Silver maple
- ✳ Gray birch
- ✳ River birch
- ✳ Sweet birch
- ✳ Yellow birch
- ✳ Beechnut
- ✳ Black walnut
- ✳ Butternut
- ✳ Elm
- ✳ Hickory
- ✳ Hop hornbeam
- ✳ Sycamore

SAP'S NOT JUST FOR SYRUP

One of my family's favorite traditions is celebrating the first tapped sugar maple of the season by sharing a glass of cold, crisp sap. This nutrient-rich beverage offers an abundance of antioxidants and electrolytes, along with the faintest hint of sweetness. So why not drink up?

Homemade Maple Sugar

Just when you think maple syrup can't get any better, you boil it down and discover that it does! That sweet amber liquid transforms into a granulated sugar right in front of your eyes. Fair warning, though: You'll need to commit to an immense amount of stirring. I prefer outsourcing this to the head of all things syruping in our house, my husband. While I like to use tired arm muscles as my excuse for not being able to stir constantly for what feels like forever, the real truth is that it comes down to patience—a lot of it. As soon as I saw the candy thermometer being pulled out of the drawer, I knew I was out. Because you are dealing with pure sugar here, watching the temperature will be your primary focus. Therein lies the key to your sweet success.

1 Pour 3 cups maple syrup into a deep pot and bring to a low boil over medium heat. You may need to either slightly increase or decrease the heat during the bubbling to prevent boilover. There is no stirring at this point, just monitoring the boil.

2 As the syrup begins to reduce, it will become dark brown (about 270°F/130°C). At this point, immediately remove the pot from the heat and place it on a heatproof board or counter.

3 The temperature will quickly drop. Keep an eye on the thermometer and grab your wooden spoon. When the temperature reads 200°F/95°C, start stirring and don't stop. Over the next 8 to 12 minutes, the syrup will begin to dry and crumble. Stir until it's completely dry. Let it cool.

4 If you'd like the sugar to be a finer grain, put it in a food processor and pulse a few times until it's the desired size and texture.

5 Time to sift. You can sift your sugar to get different-size "grains." Ours usually gets divided into three types: little sugar clusters that we use in oatmeal and granola; a coarse sugar that we sprinkle on top of cookies, muffins, and ice cream; and a granulated sugar that we use as we would regular sugar—a teaspoon adds a nice maple subtleness to morning coffee.

MAPLE-GLAZED WALNUTS

This tasty treat takes 3 minutes to whip up—almost less time than it takes to read this recipe! I'd share my favorite foods that I toss these with, but truth be told, these nuts are generally gobbled up before I have a chance to use them anywhere else.

Preheat a skillet over medium-high heat. Toss in 2 cups walnuts, ⅓ cup maple syrup, and a dash of salt. Cook for 3 minutes. If the mixture is still sticky, cook a bit longer.

MAPLE GRANOLA

This recipe makes me happy throughout the year. Whether noshed on its own with some milk, sprinkled into yogurt and ice cream, or incorporated into breads and baked goods, this maple granola just keeps me energized and satisfied all day long.

The great thing about granola is that it's so easy to customize to your taste. Omit the coconut if you're not a fan and toss in more nuts or seeds instead. After the granola has fully cooled but before you jar it up, incorporate some dried fruit into the mix if you'd like. Cranberries are a personal favorite for a little tart bite to balance the subtle sweet nuttiness.

MAKES 8 CUPS

3½	cups rolled oats
½	cup unsweetened coconut
½	cup wheat germ
1	cup chopped nuts of choice (I use ⅓ cup each walnuts, pecans, and almonds)
1	cup seeds of choice (I use ¼ cup each sunflower, pumpkin, chia, and flaxseed)
¼	teaspoon salt
½–¾	cup maple syrup (depending on how sweet you'd like it)
⅓	cup vegetable oil
1	teaspoon vanilla extract

1 Set an oven rack in the middle position and preheat the oven to 250°F/120°C. Line a large baking sheet with parchment paper.

2 Combine the oats, coconut, wheat germ, nuts, seeds, and salt in a large bowl. Whisk together the maple syrup, oil, and vanilla in a small bowl. Pour the maple syrup mixture into the oats mixture. Using clean hands, thoroughly mix until everything is well combined and the dry ingredients are evenly moistened.

3 Spread the granola in an even layer on the prepared baking sheet. Bake for 2 hours, stirring once or twice during baking.

4 Cool thoroughly and store in an airtight container for up to 1 month.

HOT SWITCHEL

This is the perfect winter warmer to sip the snow away. Heard of haymaker's punch? This is a hot take on that delicious drink that benefits digestion as it hydrates.

MAKES 2 CUPS

2   cups water
    Juice of ½ lemon
2   tablespoons apple cider vinegar
2   tablespoons maple syrup
1   tablespoon grated fresh ginger

Mix the ingredients in a small saucepan over medium heat and bring to a low boil. Reduce the heat to low and simmer for 10 minutes. Strain and sip.

Foraging from Nature's Winter Garden

Cold aside, there's something about being outside in the sparkling sun of a winter's day that makes you feel alive and invigorated. There's a stillness about the world that feels quite comforting. And while the landscape can look stark, there's still a bevy of beauties to forage.

Because we get so much snow here in Maine, our winter forage offerings aren't as vast as those in warmer climates, but there's still a lot of magic to be found. Basket in hand, I wander through our woods and along our slow country road, collecting pinecones, birch bark, snippets of Scotch pine needles, scrapings of pine resin, and many more treasures. These will become fodder for projects in the next few months, transformed into balms, cleaners, garlands, and much more.

A Birch Bark Garland

We relish all the birch we have throughout our woods. But over the years, ice storms and drought have taken their toll on some of the smaller trees, sending them tumbling to the ground— and giving us a way to harvest the striking bark. As a friendly reminder from all your tree pals, never remove bark from a living tree. Only take bark from a fallen or standing dead tree.

To make a garland, cut birch bark into strips of your desired thickness, using scissors or an X-Acto knife and a ruler. I like 2-inch-wide strips. Now just like you did as a kid making paper chains, curl the first strip into a circle and seal together with two staples. (More talented folks than I could sew it closed with red embroidery floss and a nice whipstitch.) Thread the next bark strip through that first one and staple it closed. Repeat until you reach your desired length.

NOURISH

REFRESHENING PINE TONER

For an invigorating toner that freshens dull winter skin, mix 1 cup fresh pine needles, 1 cup distilled water, and ¼ cup witch hazel. Let steep in a cool, dark place for 3 to 4 weeks. Strain and pour into a clean jar. Apply to the skin with cotton balls.

WINTER

231

A Citrus Garland

Years ago, in hopes of luring certain birds to my garden, I hung up strands of orange-slice garlands throughout my garden. Although they didn't end up attracting a single bird, they did capture my heart. Now I make several strands each winter to string not only in our woods but throughout our house, too.

When hung in draping strands across windows, these garlands will sparkle and shine like nature's stained glass. Make it twinkle even brighter by mixing in different citrus—like lemons, limes, and pink grapefruit—for a collection of colors certain to warm a winter's day.

To make the garland, slice citrus fruits into ¼-inch-thick slices and dry them in a dehydrator at 135°F/55°C. Alternatively, you can dry them in the oven. Simply place the slices on a parchment paper–lined baking sheet and bake at 200°F/95°C for about 2½ hours, until translucent.

When the citrus slices are completely dried, use a bamboo skewer to gently poke a hole large enough to thread jute string through. Guide the jute through the slices, arranging the garland to your liking.

You can make garlands that only include citrus slices, or you can mix in other natural ornaments, like pinecones and acorns. Also try tying up single citrus slices with a beautiful ribbon to hang as Christmas ornaments. You can do the same with jute string instead and hang them from tree branches outside for your bird pals. You may also find that squirrels are big fans of these sugary treats.

If you live in a dry climate, these strands will last months and months indoors. They have a shorter shelf life in more humid climates. Either way, I recommend removing them before warm weather arrives or they will attract ants.

OTHER USES FOR CITRUS PEELS

MAKE A HOMEMADE CLEANER. Loosely fill a glass jar with citrus peels (enough to fill the jar without packing the peels down), then top with a 50/50 mix of water and distilled white vinegar. Store in a cool, dark cabinet for 2 weeks, then strain into a spray bottle and get cleaning.

CANDY IT! Transform an ordinary peel into an extraordinary treat by making candied orange peels, then dipping them partway in bittersweet chocolate. Peel 2 oranges, then cut the peel into ¼-inch slices, removing any excess white pith, which is bitter. Add the peel to a pot of boiling water. Cook for 15 minutes, then drain and rinse. Combine 3 cups water with 3 cups granulated sugar in a medium saucepan and bring to a boil, stirring occasionally until the sugar has completely dissolved. Toss in the drained orange peel and bring the pan back to a boil. Reduce the heat and simmer until the peels have softened, about 40 minutes. Drain off the liquid and toss the peels with 1 cup granulated sugar. Transfer the sugared slices onto parchment paper and let sit for 2 days or until dry.

DRY IT AND GRIND IT. Dry some orange or lemon peels, then grind them in a coffee grinder until they are well flaked. Sprinkle the flakes in teas, baked goods, and seasonings of all sorts.

ADD TO HERBAL BODY PRODUCTS. Give your face scrubs and tub teas an extra boost of brightness by adding some dried ground citrus peel. It also acts as a great exfoliant.

COCKTAILS, ANYONE? Why not brew up a batch of limoncello now for refreshing summer imbibing later? Since you'll be infusing the peels in alcohol, it's best to use organic lemons so the only thing leaching in will be flavor and not pesticides.

Place the peels from about 10 lemons into a quart-size jar. Pour enough vodka over the peels to fully cover them. Place the jar in a cool, dark place for 1 month. Strain through a filter.

Prepare a simple syrup by combining ½ cup water with ½ cup granulated sugar in a small saucepan and bring to a boil over medium heat, stirring until the sugar is fully dissolved. Let cool, then add enough of the infused vodka to reach your sweet spot . . . literally. Bottle up the limoncello and store it indefinitely in your freezer.

Resources

National Gardening Association
https://garden.org

Gardening Know How
https://gardeningknowhow.com/extension-search
Find your Local Cooperative Extension Service with this search tool.

Herbal Academy
https://theherbalacademy.com

National Center for Home Food Preservation
https://nchfp.uga.edu

Index

Page numbers in *italics* indicate photos or illustrations; main entry in **bold**.